LAZARUS SPECIES

Also by Devon Walker-Figueroa

Philomath

LAZARUS SPECIES

poems

Devon Walker-Figueroa

MILKWEED EDITIONS

(800) 520-6455
milkweed.org

Published 2025 by Milkweed Editions
Printed in Canada
Cover design by Mary Austin Speaker
Cover art: *Model of Recollection IV*, oil on canvas, 2023, by Tõnis Saadoja
Author photo by David Evan McDowell
25 26 27 28 29 5 4 3 2 1
First Edition

Library of Congress Cataloging-in-Publication Data

Names: Walker-Figueroa, Devon, author.
Title: Lazarus species : poems / Devon Walker-Figueroa.
Description: First edition. | Minneapolis, Minnesota : Milkweed Editions, 2025. | Summary: "A formally ambitious second collection calculating the cost of evolution and survival"-- Provided by publisher.
Identifiers: LCCN 2025006914 (print) | LCCN 2025006915 (ebook) | ISBN 9781571315779 (paperback ; acid-free paper) | ISBN 9781571315786 (ebook)
Subjects: LCGFT: Poetry.
Classification: LCC PS3623.A359595 L39 2025 (print) | LCC PS3623.A359595 (ebook) | DDC 811/.6--dc23/eng/20250424
LC record available at https://lccn.loc.gov/2025006914
LC ebook record available at https://lccn.loc.gov/2025006915

Milkweed Editions is committed to ecological stewardship. We strive to align our book production practices with this principle, and to reduce the impact of our operations in the environment. We are a member of the Green Press Initiative, a nonprofit coalition of publishers, manufacturers, and authors working to protect the world's endangered forests and conserve natural resources. *Lazarus Species* was printed on acid-free 100% postconsumer-waste paper by Friesens Corporation.

For Justin Boening, my partner in rhyme and other mischiefs.
Without you, this resurrection would never have occurred.

Contents

I

II

I.

Eternity bores me,
I never wanted it.
—SYLVIA PLATH, "Years"

Lazarus Species

You don't even need to be born
again in order to be born against
this riddled wall, each bayonet in love
with your bare, stigmatic neck.
Strange, the worst part is the waiting
to survive. Stranger,
let's wait for the cave to act out
its name, invite the sun in
for the final rendezvous.
Oh to be you. Remember when you lived
in a century still
afeared of wild boars?
Now they march on Athens once again
to remind us how frail
our own endangerments. It's a shame. I know.
You pay someone to puncture you.
The decades whir. *Lost*
is the TV show you watch
until there's no season left
but the one caressing your window.
It's overcast. It's overkill.
Time to draw the curtains & play dead.
Once I was on a plane—
all ocean, blinding, down below—
a bald man seatbelted beside me.
He was high in every sense,
said, "I lived my father
alone to leave his life" & offered me
a hundred-dollar bill. "Here,
this is my business card.

Please stay in touch.
Please wear a toga to my funeral."
Bad enough to find yourself
in a book of vanished things,
reports of vessels gulped down
by listless seas, whole farms smuggled up
into an Oklahoma sky. Now
to be born again & still
without one ounce of faith
in the durability of anything
but silk. I took the bill
& bought myself
a used priest's robe
which I sometimes don
when I feel most prone
to survival & lament.
I, too, have not been seen
in years, so many years,
even the sycamores presumed me dead
& the boars began to dream
of meats far more exotic
than my own. Extinction is said
to be an event, but I can tell you nothing
is more uneventful—you find your family,
your whole phyla & future, buried
in some encyclopedia & glean
how small the risk of eternity,
how great the risk of not being reached for.
& under your entry, you find a man
discovered your decline & so became
famous by the standards of his day.
"There was no reasonable doubt,
the last individual had expired."

So the search for you grows
exhaustive until it dies
down & no one watches the embers
but some canceled god, retired, forgetting
his own mellifluous names. I search
for my life as well, you know,
some passing evidence
besides the noise, which drifts about me,
so much exhaust inquiring, "Is this grief
the inexactitude we'd hoped for?"

The Perch

An ancient perch has caught
my eye. He lies
intact. His scales, size of a man's
thumbnails, seem to weigh
nothing
against its all-
too-many possibilities. Inside him
(if you can make your-
self small) you'll find a hall
so huge, dead gods
must come alive
just to pass through it. I want
to pass through it—and I could
let the vast
sleeve of him swallow up
my arm in silver chain mail once alive, only
there is glass between us.
It is scratched, dusty,
smudged. The light
is dim; the air
uncirculated. After all,
however skillfully embalmed
an emblem of his kind, he is not
the main attraction:
Many gold ornaments—exhumed
from a famous pharaoh's tomb—
dwell famously
just two halls down . . . Imagine
how sparse that royal after-
life is now—no gem-encrusted throne

to host his vantage, no renderings
of slack-tongued cows to stay
his hunger, nor tiny boat
to ferry him, his age-old teenage bones,
across that memoryless realm of goings-forth
(all so we might meet
these treasures meant
only to be regarded by the dead). But remember, we are here
for the perch, who is himself
two thousand years and long carved free
of a dense pale flesh
you just might know
the taste of—I *do*
and don't. Since each perch tastes, as you'd imagine,
of his given river and his prey,
also whatever age he managed
to drift through. And though
I've stood and stared
into the archaic blue
that snakes along outside, its violent moods
now tamed by monumental
dams that kiss
both Aswan and Sudan,
I know there is no seeing
to the bottom
the perch swam along, perhaps feeling
quite safe as his long form divided
the Nile, however briefly, from itself,
as his fleet pearly belly glided close
to the fertile soil that world above
relied on for its crops—you know them well:
barley, lentil, flax, the fleshy figs,
even the thousand starlike bursting heads

of sacred reeds—as his dorsal fins
stirred the elements,
the river and its bed blurring
into each other almost tenderly
at his swaying command. Even when he surfaced,
if he did, his gold-rimmed eyes
would hardly have admired
the dry, bright heights of Thebes,
its columns standing
in ageless mimicry
of blossoming papyri. Surely,
he didn't linger *there*,
but plunged back down,
where only his kind could be schooled
in the value of his flesh, let the dark
embankments take their place
as his home's high walls. All
of this was likely finer to him
than the finest paintings
of goddess Nut, her stunning body stretched over a night
sky buried in trick passages
underground, a firmament
that hoped not to be found. Who knows
what the perch thought
of the night versus
the day, what repertoire
of threats emerged, only
to, songlike, die away, or what
feats of flight his body published
in those sparkling waters, as he established
so large an existence
in the depths, in the monumental
moment of his life. And though

he now is laid out unavoidably
as artifact, only his lack
of decay seems by design—all else,
if ordered or if artificed, was by a mind
I cannot claim to know . . .
Unlike in that other poem
you might know, there is no saving
the perch, no freeing him
from the fate of being caught
behind glass. No chance of giving
the brittle topographies of his gills
or the frail fans of his fins back
to a river that holds
no memory of nourishing him. His interior—
I'll refrain
from saying "innards," since he is more
hollow than not—
defies all logic, more
geologic in aspect than many rocks
that I have met (in these
my less-than-hallowed
three decades and a half).
And from the brief
vantage I have called my life,
I bend down toward him, craving
some grain of purchase on his age-
old Piscean view, staring as I do
into the lusterless sunken
coin that was his eye.
A fish eye, yes, it calls to mind
the type of lens that bends
the world so amorously toward it
space itself will warp

just to be held. See
the dark disc shift
in its shallow
socket two millennia ago: The perch,
not yet a captive
curio, slowly grows
large and bold and finally
curious. Now
he is glimpsing the end
of his hunger, not knowing
how long the end can last, but perhaps
registering a vague form
of freedom
descending, glinting
delicious as it angles
down, dangling
both before him and within him—
inverted, fetal, bright—
tasted by his flat-earth eye
before his mouth fills up
with its own
cold blood. Strange,
he seems to me
plated even now,
proffered to our view, as is so much
in this salmon-hued
museum full of sand-
strewn skylights. (All
of this, recall, was actually designed
by a French architect
who failed to bear
the Sahara's restless
surface in mind.) No

matter. Up river,
or even down, a line
must be snapping even now,
emitting a single note
clean as a lute's cut string,
and a fish swims off
in a tarnished flash, fleeing
the magnetic scent
of newfound pain,
while our perch keeps on
emulating sleep, along
with several other leathern lives
shelved behind this their filthy
length of glass. (Glass, I am
told, lacks "long-
range order," moving invisibly down-
ward, a solid matter longing
to be water.) A little stiff,
I have to shift my weight now,
also my eyes
from the bony perciform network of his skull—
its shifty structure free of the bizarre
articulations zippering *my* skull's plates—
down to his hindmost fins.
They look like that paper
meat comes wrapped in or pioneers
once covered windows with in place
of glass. I laugh
and lift my tongue's own
dorsal part, as if to ask, "God,
who will ever touch,
with lotus blossom and with myrrh,
the place in *us* where such huge

appetites once took place?"
True, the perch's beauty
might be called *invasive*, least
endangered and yet most
so by human hands
and water hyacinths
(also invasive, as it turns out).
No matter. Whoever,
I imagine, staved off their hunger
with the perch's heft, whoever saved
his dulled metallic skin and now-
browned bones, swabbed his skin
in the appointed unguents,
as if his body were one open
wound, whoever
gently wound him up
in linen strips
the centuries would strip away,
bound him neatly
in reeds (not picked to write
poems or decrees), did they mean
for us to see him or
was the idea that he *too* would pass
into an eternity
where only our hungers survive
us? Where his ghost could feed
the ghost of some young pharaoh
finally impoverished,
immortal, free? It harrows me to weigh
the possibilities, the way
his body must have flashed almost synaptic
in that liquid rage
of void, his movements indivisible

from what he felt. The glass, too,
continues to concern me—
smudged as it is
with what seem great efforts
to reach through it. Why won't the museum
do something—clean it up, swap it out
with a pane less easily marked?
Then again, there are so many hours
when the perch's legibility matters not
at all, at night, say,
when the halls are purged
of pilgrimage and language,
and the shadows, crouched
under their given
artifacts, begin to bloom
outward till they touch
and mix and stunningly displace
the artifice of daylight, all at once
emptying the displays
of *contrast*. Even the walls
most rapturous with history
must then be wrapped in that sensual
atmosphere of infinite negation . . .
The perch, though, he is not
concerned. His body holds its shape
while I behold
it however awkwardly, raising
and lowering my head, bobbing
as if in place to catch the best
glimpse of his naked,
nacre-like immensity: the slippery
syntax of his rearmost blushing scales;
his skin, thin as the gilt

fussily dabbed on an antique
page's edge; then come the splayed
blades of his ribs; the belly
hollow as a harp, yet full
of that ilk of emptiness
all music requires to live . . .
But now I am caught
off guard by a woman's finger
prying deeply into me, my back. How long
have I been blocking
her view? Her gesture throws me
off-balance: I throw a hand
against the intervening plate
of glass, adding to it
my own unholy oils. Our eyes meet
because our words can't. And anyway,
hasn't she already spoken
with the part of her that bends
most readily into a hook—
reminding me the meat
of me cannot stay here? No. Cannot stay
perched between its own
reflection and the gaping
mummy fish that swam in time-
lapse through twenty centuries
of conquest and collapse,
who might in fact have passed,
during flood times, through sand-
stone temples, darting past
the at last moistened eyes
of Isis—all this—just to nourish
a stranger's desire to see me
disappear. But I don't *want* to go.

And only as I resurface to a world
of hours and appropriate
moments we can spend communing
with an arti-
fact whose whole form seems
one dusty scar, do I glance down
at a small white plate, barely legible
through all the glass's glaring flaws, half
written in my tongue, half
in the more incurvate script
of Arabic: *No traces of the original*
bandaging remain
from this Nile perch.
And from my imperiled angle,
I read on, to find the perch was not
eaten at all. Not even tasted. No.

Glossolaliac

the confusion of tongues is no longer a punishment
—ROLAND BARTHES

For he that speaketh in an unknown tongue speaketh not unto men,
but unto God.
—SAUL OF TARSUS

I.

Your gift visits my other-

wise repulsive tongue, the face's gate

          hinging sans per-
mission mine: I babble, trouble
the rapid eye

movements of gods, move them to voice

a cave, a flood, a florid

constellation aspiring to be

a wagon or a bear

               devoid of vice.
Can disgust catalyze

                    the speech of clouds?

Look: They part,
                    impart light.

II.

It's an enviable state—to serve

as chaos's entrance
into a room, entrance the room

with a lament meant to abscise
syllable from sound. This

languid age I halve into what

I call dead and not-
            yet-born might yet

be viable. Centuries go by, rank
and vile, filed

            yet alive, and still
I find no forgiveness

cradled in my Lord-
storm's wagon. Imagine
            a sure hand grasping

a wheel, wild waters parting,

the hand portending blind-

folds and fortunes ended
by the sea. If nothing is
the surrogate

for fear, I'll go   in fear. And if

an elated deity no longer needs

company, I'll seek
to displease

at the highest levels; I'll tend
to godly needs by being *anything*

but good. I've discussed
this matter with the dust,

whose antecedent I am
ceding to a swelling

sea. But back

to the Cradle of Civil—

III.

Disobedience and the fruit, you mentioned.
Also the plenitude of being, and I

so precisely misunderstood
when you asked, "You know

what I mean?" I can't

know, so I incant
to no one, am slated

to translate what can't be mutated
                    nor muted out

                                        of mystery, be
mutilated nor made

unearthly whole. Join me.
Rise. Let's hymn

and hymn until the sentence escapes
its fiery landscape and

us and even the word *virus* is

as a clapper striking its dome
of brass, of bone. Call me in-

                    sincere. Call me
to the wall that's always been waiting

for us,   for purpose. I'll pose

against it, make of my guilt
a guardian; I'll paint

                    a gate on it
with my red fingertip, tip-

toe through it and instigate
a marriage of bliss and fear.

(ō   ō   ō   ō)

(Mind + end = mend,   I fear.)

IV.

If our Lordstorm didn't intend
to end up a legend, I can

pull a banquet from a horse's ear.

My guess: He knew his story
would replace him. My guest,

his escapades and daydreams were hardly
greater than your own: to build a home

in the mountains, to make up

a mind, to wield the weary weather

when it suited him. Tender me a fool, but the first
time I read the word

Sumer, I thought it a perversion
of *summer*, some other

version of the sun's pre-
meditated rampages. I say.

it's been ages since we've held

each other. You say
your name, which is hidden

within me: Enlil. Ama. Jackie. Jack.
I turn rosy and turn a page

filled with gutless strings that sing

silence and lose

the thread of our conversion, our con—

V.

Here I am, cadaverous
in the mind, infantile in the real

City of Unlifted Eyes. Here
I go, an inversion of a person

I once trusted more than I
do the fact of birth, the rustle

of illuminated sheets, the tremor
a siren threads through heads.

My metaphysics have gone
cold, my bold voice

quiet as a root's
reaching. And what I deem

humble is profligate, given
the correct opportunity. So size

me up. Surprise me
with your rearranged smile,

with your forgiveness deranged

as a zephyr. I'll be looking for milk-
blooded bulbs to synaesthetize us into

trances, give us transit
from site to site to parasite. I'll be looking

to relate us to a future you tell
what to do. What to do.

(The sky loses   weight, wets
this tied and upturned tongue.)

VI.

Give me a hint. Hunt

my reply. Help me to live

up to your illusions, the ones that stray

until ill. (I'll live down

the ones that don't.) The story was never

meant to be palatable or
relatable. Extend me

the courtesy of survival. Distend me

with a dropseed untended

as manna or as man. I will curtsy
my proper humiliation, de mon propre.

Madame V, of the Kirov
Ballet, once bent my spirit

and feet like coat hangers meant
to pick locks. She laughed

the while. I drafted
my revenge in a quiescence potent

as absinthe. I am
stories half-told like the rest of us.

We are stories half-told
like the rest of me.

I revise the future, throw a discus

like a die, and wash my hands.

(Sigh.)

VII.

The dirt conjugates our sentence.
The dirt hates our spent tenses.
The dirt eats our sentient chances.
The dirt bleeds us a conscience.
The dirt leads us to sighs and stances.
The dirt depletes us into stanzas.
The dirt pleats us into science.
The dirt deletes from us our senses.
The dirt completes our senseless.
The dirt contemplates our intenseness.
The dirt templates our scenes listless.

Blissless, the dirt runs its mouth.

VIII.

Can we pronounce the light
guilty of what it holds? What it solves but doesn't
save? I wanted once to blame the flaming bulb

that loomed over the room in which I lost
my bliss, but I couldn't bring myself
to anything but pity, which a wise man

once told me is a form
of condescension. And, so, I descend,
and tend my mouth. I worship

the storm that worships my lowliness,
the lord that says my poverty is good,
and it is good, even if it is the end

of me, even if it is the burning
bush that eavesdrops on my mind.
Flammivomous and ageless voyeur

who would have me know a lack
of privacy is proof of love. I think
and am not redeemed, demeaned

by demoniacal listening: I sing
to the storm that started me: Worry,
my lord, this world is

the last thing you will see.

Australopitheca[1] & Starman[2]

10

The countdown to you begyns w/ me, deere Starman,
when I wander, dumbly, deep into a space hospittable
to Hunger. Now, all's desert. No milk in syte. Just pitifull
sand, what shushes as it slydes through your hande
to rejoin itself. I'd join myself with a stellar human
who, as you do, dons whyte suits & travells light, is able
to drive all seasons w/ the top down & tell me terrible
jokes. If you kin keep yr posture in the face of bad demands,
I promise to objectively vivify you, insofar as the dead
can keep a promise. As for me, the last thing I sawe
wasn't Earth, but a domed desert littered with fyres
I could read. Its sands emulated the colore of the dead
center of your eye, the part that ceaselessly seizes awe,
puts it inside the future's fossil, & plaies it like a lyre.

1. "Australopitheca," otherwise known as "Lucy," is an incomplete *Australopithecus afarensis* fossil & a forerunner to *Homo sapiens sapiens.*

2. "Starman" is the name of the dummy who currently sits in the driver's seat of a Tesla Roadster traveling through outer space, after having successfully exceeded escape velocity on February 6, 2018. It has been theorized that he may collide with Venus, Earth, or the sun in the distant future.

9

You're inside the future, a fossil played like a lyre.
I think you're like me, lonely passenger. In this skye
devoid of diamonds,[3] call me Lucy. Call me high
or low: All turns truthfull at the right remove. I admyre
your bravado & carriage, Starman, how you retire
from orbit just to drive Mars mad. Like a note tied
to a tongue, you holde on, but aren't helled; & empteyed
of the earthshadow you move through, you aspyre
to exit similitude; but I'm your likeness & an interlude
of asteroids lies ahead.[4] We'll collide, 'lide time, tremble
in a treble only troubled seraphs dare perceive. 6 billion
years & every ostinato turns to torture, love, & lewd
dance moves fade to formes of piety. I'd disassemble
dystance just for you, man, to humble these mean eons.

3. Lucy was found in Ethiopia's Awash Basin in 1974. Her name was taken from The Beatles' song "Lucy in the Sky with Diamonds," which had been playing loudly and on loop at the dig site on the day the fossil was first discovered.

4. Starman is at risk of passing through an asteroid field and being obliterated.

8

Distance lusts for you, Starman, & crumbles us lean peons
like sunneflowers, faces singed under the face that feedes
their leaving—flamesource of ligule, hilum, seed.
I, Lucy, am a sorceress fashioned from bone, sapless pawn
only in my *own* hands. When they dug me up, my breede
was mysterie. They brushed dust from my spyne; my feete
they deemed feeble but able to forge their way.[5] Dawn
of man, they said; spawn of music, malady, & a fervent need
for True. I'm no ape of Pindares. Like you, to be free's
my naturall state & the end of me, an enemy who won
me over: Sure, I turned my mind toward proving the invisible
a fraud, horizon's sad accomplice & refrayne. Now, degrees of
remove prove you wonderfull; &, against my will, love
augments & empties my tune: Are you, too, invincible?

5. The shape of Lucy's pelvic bone indicates that she was bipedal, though lacked arches in her feet.

7

Your mute argument turns my head; & I remayne divisible
in the face of your flammivomous exodus: makes me think
forever's a fever that just won't break. You might thank
me for my preternatural patiens, Starboy, my inner villain's
prudance: I'd anneal you w/ cunning contumelies! In vain,
I admit: What curse could turn your course from the brink
of the effable? What fable turn yr head? The dead do rank
you highly among young mummies; & the living explaine
you away as an inventor's red right hand, gloved in a plane's
matter. Much belov'd in yr high gloss sarcophagus & drunk
on a planet's calando applause, you lack a plan; so young
you are compared to the fission diminishing in yr rearview;
& so unworried by the crisp husk falling out of yr purview.
Of Course I Still Love You[6] gathers up yr glittering junk.

6. *Of Course I Still Love You* is an autonomous spaceport drone ship in the Atlantic Ocean whose purpose is to recover multistage rockets' first stages. In parallel staging schemes, rocket boosters are added to create the requisite force for liftoff. These parts, necessarily shed, are sometimes called "stage 0." OCISLY's precursor is *Just Read the Instructions* and its follow-up model is *A Shortfall of Gravitas.*

6

Of course I still love you & your grande, annihilatory junket
threading epochs. Like Cupido's deft arrow borrowéd
from Time itself, you prick a void & bring me to my knees.
Nothing dilates. Then Everything cracks like a joke wed
to a wound. There's laughter living under your mirrored
helmet, but who can hear it? Not you, with the weird frets
of your guts, yr hands at 10 & 2, yr bespoke seedcoat.
Something is wrong. Anything boring is terrible.[7] Don't
panic. I'm frequenting origin's frequency. Or please
pan to Mars, who awaits yr scattered touch, my maquette
so bacterial.[8] Earth in 2018's not a planet I call myne, nor
you yours. Yes, "Earthling" used to mean nothing more
than "farmer." Now it speaks a point of view we don't want
to imagine is ours. You're alienating me, man + rocket.

7. "Test flights of new rockets usually contain mass simulators in the form of concrete or steel blocks. That seemed extremely boring. Of course, anything boring is terrible [. . .] so we decided to send something unusual, something that made us feel."—Elon Musk, via Instagram

8. Because the Tesla Roadster and its passenger were not held to the same standards of sterilization to which NASA launches are held, some scientists at the time of Starman's launch expressed concern that he could one day collide with another planet, such as Mars, and introduce foreign bacteria, a potential catastrophe for native microbes.

5

You're relineating your maddest scene where no one can
scan it, Rocketman. I'd like to hum along, but divisibility's
key in this ruptured plea bargain: enter infinite probability,
our shared gift horse. Why not gallop to our end? Press
Send & kiss gravity hello? Oh, I know it can't allways bee
romantic & grave, but I'd attempt to glean your moode, plan
for a stretch of *will-have-been* & *would,* if only I could address
you less intensely. So a planet's antique feares re-dress
you in leaves, leave yr Nothing to a universe's imagination.
& somewhere, an old intelligence distills leonine nations
down to their ions. & somewhere else, a thin theory forges
our forgetfullness all over again, fusing Charm & Strange
quarks, their glue[9] quickbreeding into a blue, simulated orgy
of departure & bliss. But look: The mythic net holding
you warps gorgeously.

9. Referring to the gluon binding energy that holds quarks together.

4

Think of archers blitzed, of telescopic muzzles
                                        arming an army of eyes that shoot
you through till you careen beyond their reach, unthreaded
by all seeing save mine, save yours—True & yet true, I broode,
having layne down in my bed of unbegun plants, plans, & dreaded
records that skip at every planetary turn. There is no food
I have not learned to fear, man, no drop of nectar un-indebted
to some god who'd slap it from my trap. But here's the hard sell:
If you loop back round like a well-tuned boomerang, the plenum
will greet you; mimic Time's Arrow, tho, & you'll go full numb.
Sorry to tread so heavily, Starboy, tho I lack feet, tho I'm seldom
subject to rotation or regret. Here in the museum of my life, my cell
might well be empty—filled w/ priceless crumbs, these my numerous
remaynes feigning calm. Come home. We'll be numinous; & yes,
sigh & prophesy our need . . .
    to leap from fortune's dirty carousel.

3

Tell me why we mimic colossi & cleave dirt, yet carouse
w/ what a lemniscate attempts to represent? I sent
me out one day to end my thirst & to repent, was spent
by distance & divided by time. Nothing could arouse
me for millennia. Then you came along, w/ yr pent
smile. Tell all: Will an asteroid belt riddle yr frame? Will it bend
you to its will as if you're light & it were gravity? Rows
gravid w/ xanthic ears fail to reseed their earthly selves
this year, while I recede beneath my swarm of offspring,
who stand in lyne & wait for the last encorps of spring.
A whale composes a planh. A kid claps her face shut to say,
"It's *my* fault," then looses a melodious plea into the vault.
& nobody's best guess, at last, proves good enough to stave
off a re-run of odious glands. Go on: Cue the light Vivaldi.

2

I offer you my far-flung glance, imbue my cries, however bald,
w/ charm. No harm, young shaman, in showing yr cupidity,
nor in confessing, say, the source of your galactic quiddity's
my climb up fruitfull trees to capture the future's sprawled
imagination. Even when mad, I mind the image of you mauled
by a skirmish w/ comets, their tails rich w/ finitude quitting
you of your head, which, like any mummy's, is all in the fitting
of its pale wrapper. Rapturously ruptured, the sky goes piebald
with imploding Pleiades in the arousing *then*, in my anthem
of extinction. Please reply. Are you yet, Starman, among gods?
Has not a luminous arrow helped you see a tree flee toward
her own becoming? Slave to seasons, I'm reduced to a thought
thawed into a ritual of affliction & greenery, till you give word
from yr zodiacal zoo, yr tomb festooned in cosmic speleothems.

1

Can you learn to love the specimen known to men as AL 288-1?
From yr tumid dome; yr doomed pit; yr home to mad, nomadic
flames; why would my brief prehistory entice you? That vatic
void you drift thru is yr one & lonely understudy; & if I've won
at anything, it's loss. Yes. What we're sentenced to is *so long* & won't
regret its medium is exile. So, hold yr tongue, pregnant w/ static;
fold your arms round the nothing that so becomes you, sticks
to your ribs like a tick taking its time. To talk it out wasn't a want
I harbored. (Hushed, I wished to be harlequinned, a queen invalid
who inspires travel & saccharine secretions.) Granted, certain
dreams draw harm. Granted, my most opposable digits entertaine
only a faulty grip & apish aptitude for risky pilgrimage. I lied
when I told you I was young. You lied w/ silence, as yr puppeteers pillaged
my grave out of boredom. Now I'm here, laid out for the ages.

0

Even our lips got carried away, pink pilgrims so odd & assuaged
in their coliseum of ether. Musick imbued us w/ decadence,
made us reel. Then an animal ate my heart out, its cadence
turned to sweet repast; & you were mocked up madly, an image
smeared over a force field, forced into a life of grim homage.
I think yr spaceship doesn't know the way home.[10] Some density
unfigured in the formula & Nothing to be done. So, the orisons
exit stage left, desert us as if they were origins, while the last page
turns on itself for good. Make it count, love. Flaunt yr caparison
made of light, that I might take its hem between my teeth. The sunn
is lapping at a newborn's still-sealed eyes. To follow: the azure
that will one day disappoint it. I was once translated into a sure-
footed thing, still full of noise & disappearance. By-&-by, immured
in my mind & Nowhere, you are

beside yourself.

10. "And I think my spaceship knows which way to go" is a line from David Bowie's "Space Oddity," which is playing on an infinite loop in Starman's Roadster.

Crown Shyness

The ends Crowne our works, but thou crown'st our ends,
For, at our end begins our endlesse rest.
—JOHN DONNE, "La Corona"

why do you choose me, when to choose is to break?
—A SHADE IN THE WOOD OF SUICIDES, Dante's *Inferno*

Even the trees are afraid of losing their breath. The forest
won't touch itself, won't close the distance written blue
between its fingers. (We haven't got a prayer it hasn't tried, naked with waiting
for a daughter to come home.) A daughter, I look down instead of up
but still hear plastic bags trade secrets in the network overhead.
Maybe God is just, in the end, the feeling of being ceaselessly

watched. People keep their faces to themselves, move away
as I come close. Ghosts ghost their covered mouths
to join the weather's frigid ritual— while the sidewalk states,
in letters big as hands, "HI, KNAVE." I wave and feel the words
watch me step onto them. So wild we call it stiff, the wind conveys
an orphaned mask across an orphaned street, while the yogini who made her living
instructing us to breathe—to hold and hold and hold

a pose called "corpse," called "plough," called "tree"—finds herself
talking to the dead as she walks past vast white trucks releasing
low *oms* into the siren-shot night. (Picture the freight
as many red carnations and chocolate pudding cups, any perishable
the sick might like.) *All changing unchang'd Ancient of days,* I say to see

a line of fog infecting the frigid dusk, vectoring on
through a dormant crown that looks for all the world

like the vasculature creaking   inside us—Yes
and No are all   its branches (wind-heaved, heavy) seem to say.
Clang! Clang!   A neighbor beats the cymbals of his pans,

meaning the day is finally over itself, *the first*   *last everlasting day—*
seven to summon a world, fourteen   to kill a curve
in a welbelov'd imprisonment   stocked with Tylenol and tea. And no one
comes and goes   from the pixel of her studio
without first scanning a lone   passage lit with "EXIT" at one end. Recall the blood-

red light throbbing into white   at four a.m. The lost
wages, tunes, ambivalence, and scents   (butter left unlidded in the sun, last season's
bunched asclepiads   turned downy and perfumeless on the sill). Found:
The word "curve"   is cousinly to "crown" and "crow"
as the strains we're catching   on to sans much choice. And all this time, and
all this time, the man I love can't catch   his breath, Emergency's just the name

of another room that can't swallow our panic,   and there's talk
of sowing local parks   with yesterday's incarnations—
who must await further instructions.   (Just a thought, we're told. Shallowest
of burials. But I need to *know*:   What was the closing
thought before each life lay down   its humble metronome, and the coroners slit
the coronated lungs to sing   "scorched earth" on the nightly news?)

Thank you for holding.   *We are experiencing an unusual volume* . . . of senses
hypoxic with hope. Again,   a call warms the ear with waiting;
one's place is lost in the complete   Donne; and all relations, like positions, grow
remote as the bright pretense of makeup.   Call to mind

not a renaissance   of palms daubed red, but the impending
green *Which cannot die, yet*   *cannot chuse*   *but die,* shy host
to insect sounds, bold shade   that crowns each summer
in a victory of leaves (whose breathing keeps   trading places with our own)

[Horns Within]

I too have studied
deserving, served myself
dessert six times a week
when I thought of fathers
as a heavenly breed
of ghost. Now I care more
for snails, the brittle helices
they haul over the dirt, the thin
mucosal lines they trace
in cursive on my windows
late at night (like a pledge
or curse, a blessing or a poem
about sex). I get them
as a sylph gets the air or a jester
the errors of kings. Sometimes
while getting nailed
I think about them, how it's not
really their fault
the sun can touch them
to death, how instead
of feathers to lift them
into a great confusion
of blue, their coat of spit
fuses them to earth, refuses
to let the tongue of them
taste too much
beyond the dirt. It occurs
to me their horns are
sightly when extended: Sticky
as anthers, tender

as fingertips, they rise & fall
in a private largo. Once,
when the moon was glued
high up in its vault
of indigo, I pressed my breasts
against the pane the snails
adhered to like a law. They
traveled over me, not even noting
the nothing that I donned. "Why not
put me to use?" I asked them.
"Make of me a public, tell
your tales of falling
so deep inside your cargo!
Or how coolly you cure
the rose bush of its blooms
before you're dipped in butter!"
At this, one lifted its near-
translucent head, let spread
the ruffles of its wet foot. Another
flared its one lung, pressed
a jelly eye against the glass.
Any other time, I would have left
the window latched, as drafts
leave me uneasy, but I was
woozy with a need that night to inch
it open, watch
that slick procession of recluses traverse
my window sill & then discharge
themselves onto my unmade bed.
They wanted to procure me.
I knew that much. I knew
by their failure

to speak up. They slid
gradual as dawn
over my sheets, their paths marked out
in drool-ish threads, then rose
in spirals up my calves,
my trunk, my neck & narrow
chin with its vague cleft.
They climbed & climbed,
conspired & grew terribly
thirsty till they found the more
obscure parts they sought out.
First came the complication
of the ear, too small
a hall for grown-up shells
to pass through. Then the mouth,
its lips through which they slipped,
pretty as sin. They clung
to the roof, the budded tongue,
the blushing crypts
of tonsils, only to lose
interest & go down
the dark hatch to find
a bed of leaves & over-
seasoned leftovers. The snails
sit heavy on my stomach,
I confess, mock
me from within, but it's not
their fault. They still write me
letters of a kind, cursing
any father who'd sing
his daughter past asleep. I think the world,
& likely always will,

of snails. They tell me
to tell the rose bush
how to die. They tell me
they could never
leave me as the daylight does.

C. Elegans

A neurosurgeon tells me, the present is only the remembered present,
and daylight is just the god-of-eight-minutes-ago. I take his word as present.

I split a thought between my nails and think it's Adam. Then I fall
out with myself, begin to chart my life's logarithmic
decline along the Y- axis, gird my thin skin in pretense.

My motor cortex fires before I know I'm going to move my mouth,
my foot, my crooked index finger. The implication is grave
or not: The brain knows before the mind—every thought pre-sent.

Consider the male nematode whose gut glows blue when life is running
low, the iridescent dye a language relaying
quietus to corpuscle (though this parlance dims
six hours after death itself presents).

Yesterday, I was bad obsessed with a man whose brain I witnessed
sliced thin as prosciutto, placed between sheets of glass. He teaches me
two kinds of memory, two kinds of present tense.

There's a sea- horse shaped part of every person that, if taken
away, makes her synthetic
Zen, takes each synapse past perfect into present sense.

I attempt to potentiate the long-term, though my recall's in decline—a has-been
since before I knew my mind was inelegant. No matter,
I still have my stage presence.

My Madness Is My Love Toward Mankind

—for Nijinsky

People are mistakes and I
do not want to commit any. Opinions
are in me. God is in me. More
than anything, immobility is
an invented thing. I have two ends
and they are both on fire. Because I am alive,
I do not like the bygone centuries.
Because I am alive, swallows flee
at the sight of me. Exaggeration
is not in me, nor the will to kill tsars,
nor to live in the streets, nor to live
in men. (The war never stops
to think of me.) In order
to earn money, I will part
soon. I kiss my hands. I do not want
a scene, nor the death of senses,
nor any policy of wanting. I
eat meat, long for a streetwalker, and beg
the people, after I am killed, to start a war
in which I am the only casualty.
Cats scratch my soul and the stars
do not say good evening to me.
I shout Death! and stand
on my head so the public understands me.
They like to be astonished, ruin the Stock
Exchange and my nervous system.
I do not like their God. He loves me

only after I provide Him with the means
of existence. All over
the world, I flew an airplane and cried in it.
I smelled out the poor and pretended to be mad.

The Peasant's Orgasm

Three clear orbs fall across the blue edge
of my vision. Frail neural fables the retinae chase
after, I want to say, but can't quite
catch. Meaning,
I fail to follow
the orbs' trajectory (so often my own
thinking too) until these odd geometries
exit the visual
field. I asked my husband's coworker once,
out of the blue, over
a business dinner,
what his consciousness felt like to him. His thoughts. I mean,
I said, is it colors ribboned with speech or
some other tumble of sensations
equally hard to articulate?
(Those aren't the words I used
exactly, but you catch my meaning. I
mean, my drift.) He was so delighted
to be assigned
the impossible—to describe the clouds
of qualia crowding his brain case—
that he never resumed his discussion of loss
leaders, which in their way
have an operatic ring, though one that perishes
quickly in the corporate
lingo his tongue was freighted with. I got the sense
my asking him about his private
self—I mean, interiority—
its ineffable and peculiar
quality, led him ultimately from pleasure

to rage, though, which he soon directed
toward my husband. My husband,
who lovingly calls this man
"Hole." I can't confirm
the causal chain,
but out of his reveries, his healthy
reverence for his own mind, Hole—
who donned a hand-knit carmine cap—leapt
at my husband's proverbial throat,
quite out of the blue, near yelling
in a rather upscale Italian joint
in DUMBO, under the distended shadow
of that huge foreshortened bridge, *You know so much*
about language, but you don't know, not yet
anyway, the language of Design. The implication
being that Hole knew
the language of Design,
that Mars and Saturn and Jupiter were just
characters in a larger alpha-
bet my husband (also, I) could never read.
I'm of course exaggerating,
but the exaggeration feels true,
the way the northern lights do
even though they're pure
distortion. A silence
then settled briefly
over the table, effecting the quality of precipitation
—I mean, snow—when it can be said
to sublimate, while Hole's anger dissolved into the din
of diners—wine-drenched laughs, the delicate symphony of forks touching plates,
low murmurs suggestive of privacy and futility,
which reminds me of the perpetual inversion
haunting the plate

at the back of the eye. The world served
forever up
like a slaughtered cow hung high to drip-
drip-
drip, and yet—
without preparation and wholly
beyond the reach of appetence, with its untold
motivational force
akin to that of pain
and the orgasm—devoured by the eye
before the mind can even hunger for it. Somehow
the conversation resumed while I was blipped out (toggling
between scenes
of chilly butcheries and subway cars, rib cages
of various life forms dangling
from metal rods), and the men
were now discussing matters
of taste, which seemed more appropriate to me than accusation, although
every discourse on taste is also a way of tasting the other's
system of scrutiny. Fonts fell
under scrutiny. The sacredness
of some,
the profanity of others, and how
fonts could be paired
like certain meats are to fine wines. I wanted to know the fate
of Garamond, which I like best, for the almost "world" that closes
its utterance. My husband favors Futura, and I forget
Hole's preference, though if I had to guess
I'd go with Helvetica.
It was only the first course,
and I wanted to reach under the table and do something obscene,
instigate, with a strategic touch, a timeless
sculptural desire in my husband, the way I used to do

to summon him, quite out of the blue,
into back-alley sex acts,
but my fingers felt bled of all strategy. I mean, intent. And I started to smell the tang
of blackberries as they shift
from fruiting to hoarding
carbohydrates in their roots,
and I saw the far-off fields
I grew up in overwrite
empire and dinner and the urban longing for what can no longer be retrieved
in its midst—the texture of clay-rich dirt
under my nails, all of it
crushingly sun-warmed and unlanguaged. Taste the grapes
whose insides would be forced
into rich flavors of oblivion
sommeliers might describe as "notes
of loam and asparagus" . . . swished and swirled
in a concurrent new-world
Italianate scene, though interred
under a rich layer of presence, the grapes pressed, in a future
now passed, by someone who will have been in possession
of the requisite million-
dollar press capable of translating fruit
into pleasure, if not
addiction and civility, whole Kalapuyan regions compressed into lines
curling over menus in New York. (To sell possibility
must be enough, those who designed me
taught me. To grow
the grapes, even if you have no means
of crushing them, is a living. Every peasant I've ever been or known
knows this truth.) Distraction
more than seduction being my
métier, I asked them both, feeling I might fortify their strained bond,
if either one of them were going to order

the rabbit because, if not, I would have to order it myself.
But this is wrong.
The memory is out of order.
Long before the yelling and the lustful soil came the rabbit.
Before the rabbit,
or long after it had been eaten
by Hole, I described, wholly off-topic, a course
I wanted to teach, called Wrong Science,
in which my students and I would digest untruths
that had entered this world in a diction of certitude
and with all the ineluctable fervor
of revelation. We would take turns
looking through the lead tube
of an early telescope,
watching the sun orbit our infancy,
suspecting
a distillation of all evil
to be crouched under our feet
instead of the lavatic rituals and shifting plates
the future, now the past, would finally acknowledge. You
could include a section on vision,
Hole suggested, and talk about mantis shrimp,
how they see all these colors we can't,
colors we used to assume didn't exist. But
how can we assume the absence of something whose presence we can't even begin
to imagine? My husband answered, nostalgia
for the Garden or
the future, and then edited himself: future nostalgia.
And long before that, the longing for someone to ask, but not with words,
what is your thinking?
And what does it feel like
to hold its happening inside you?
In the middle distance imperceptible to language?

And why did you lie as a child
when asked if you saw ghosts, going so far
as to describe them as perfect
circles drifting through inner space,
by which you meant, the sky?
Someone, over dessert, dark
chocolate torte or maybe it was buttered artichoke, changed
the subject
to Egypt's Middle Kingdom, the gaudy
shades of its presiding architecture—picture
the desert dabbed
with reds and golds and toxic-looking blues, the towering
implausibly pigmented likenesses of gods
who levied taxes and slew their serpent brothers.
I grew excited.
Hole lifted his wine glass to his mouth.
And it was red.
My husband was trying to chew and swallow
his cocktail's greenish garnish, a leathery lime slice
dusted in orange pepper, and this made me fall
in love with him all over again, his curiosity that etiquette can never conquer. His incorruptible
appetite for what may or may not be
digestible. All to say,
while the men replenished, I tried to describe a moment I'd never lived in,
when slaughter came to be
replaced—however nominally—by artistic representation,
as though the image had always been annihilation's aptest understudy, just waiting
in the celestial wings,
and the buried pharaohs finally learned, deeply
as computers lately do, that meat carved with a stylus into a wall
kept far from worldly sight was far more tender
and delicious

than meat whose rot inevitably offered
a not wholly satisfying rhyme to their own. Digestion is also a form
of decay, my husband noted
somewhere along the line. And a movement
in architecture, Hole added, that's concerned
with adaptation to shifting conditions. I noted
the care and strategy with which the tongues were often carved,
hanging from the cows' mouths so the dead would not mistake for ornament
their perennial sustenance. The Greek influence
is so strong there, Hole might have said. You can see it best
in Alexandria. So I hear. All those archives
burning in fevered minds. History lost
in flames we can no longer read
or warm our hands by. Of course,
all of that's likely fiction. The burning,
that is. A conquer so sudden and luminous it couldn't even be seen
until it was over. Now they're saying it was numerous fires spread
out over time. The conversation veered
to Plato then, as Socrates always knew it would, as he paced
the hemlock deeper into his dilating veins
while my future mouth watered at the thought.
I might've been that rare symposiast
who was also a woman, I ventured, uncertain
what shapes really related to what whirred
like alien weather behind my eyes. It's true,
my husband verified. She's a harpist—and former
bartender. She would have been allowed.
I could have poured the wine
and plucked the strings, I said. I could have
accompanied you.
So music transcends category, Hole said excitedly. I mean, gender. As in music
can pay your passage
to forbidden

places. Parties. Underworlds. Lives beyond life. I used to want to live forever
until I realized eternity would mean losing
everything anyway, the slow decay
of the wonderful, time digesting mystery
and misery like the same stale piece of cake, all of joy
and its aching origins and taxons
turning to dust in the grasp
of your ancient and unmurderable
mind. Space dust, my husband might have said. Space
as dust. Dust as mote or motive, I said. Yes.
It would be like witnessing your essence—
I mean, your whole soul—consumed
by what . . . all the distances inside it coming to
constitute it. Or
something . . . At the table next to ours a woman was discussing
monetizing her personality. Or maybe it was her lifestyle.
So many likes, she said,
on that skydiving post. Air thrumming in her ears, confiding
such elusive velocities. I want to say
it was something like three hundred.
More. A peasant skydiving in an alternate
century, growing so literate in distance and its breathtaking closure
that kings down on Earth began to swoon,
their gilded pleasure eclipsed
by a would-be swallow's. I want to say
I'm remembering correctly,
that my husband did in fact order the hare.
Or maybe it was the coniglio.
That the same flesh passed over the two men's tongues
though tasted of different animals because the tongues were divergent as were their fields
of blushing buds
and words. As for me, I forget the taste of
that night, and the more I reach for it, the less existent it becomes. So I look up

the orbs. It turns out they're a sign
of detachment, the vitreous humor lifting . . .
"a sign," the page I'm reading says, "of aging." So I look up
at the orbs. As they fall—I mean, drift—
they lighten the bit of blue
they pass over. And lose dimension. Frail triad of contact
lenses descending through space
at the pace of snow
through the lower atmosphere. But I've seen these things
for as long as I can remember.

Ode to "Your Majesty"

Entre los labios y la voz, algo se va muriendo.
—PABLO NERUDA, "Poema XIII"

On your cap is a crown & a coat
Of arms, Your Majesty, on which is etched
A majuscule B wreathed
In lobed leaves that believe
They are ribbon. I roll you up. My lips cease
To lack your precise
Lacquer. I agree to be
An animal on which you're tested
Out for beauty. You taste of crayon—
Shade of brick I chewed
Up as a child. As a child,
I smashed your ancestor all over
My face, then subtracted my face
From the mirror, watched my mouth—
Color of you—stay behind. Your Majesty,
My third-grade teacher, who liked flamingos
Too much, warned me you were born
Out of the suffering of bunnies & before
That from the slaughter of scale
Insects that suckled cactus palms.
They were all female & crushed
& wanting to be worn.
I want to be worn, Your Majesty, but down
Like the braille in a well-loved book.
I have never loved
That film *The Andalusian Dog*
For the bisected eyeballs that live

Inside its spooled reel. I fear losing
These spheres I hold you with. Your Majesty,
Never lose yourself to me.
I can say this with my other tongue
& it sounds like a song.
Your Majesty, may I sing to You?

Ameliorates

Am rote, am rot, more
marl tiara, less
toil to rate irate, am
Rita, loiterer aerial,
amrita to me, atrial
till ill, illiterate at trial,
am lit, am lore or rite,
trite? less elite, lame
meteorite, loamier
mère, arm-to-arm, mere
rialto, remote
or mote, less
ètoile, so-so liar,
mortal tamale, Team
Alto—la la, oral
lariat, more
aroma, less ram, am
alert, I err, I ate, lit
oil met roar, me—
am slit, am to aerate,
mile-to-mile am too
real to rat, mail lotto
to Ma, more aerolite,
less marital, sell trill
to remit time, rime,
too late to tire, am
ire REM-less, oarless,
oatless, amoral, am
mitral, amidol, am

tailor, atelier, aim?
to eat meat, trail
time, eat lime, lie still,
still lame, I'm all
mate, máter, matter,
more material

As a Prisoner for the Lord, Then, I Urge You to Live

You're one step away   from forfeiting
your turn at reason. Convention's just another name
    for strategy when you see   fit to tame my confusions.

I can see I've shuffled   your feathers. I mean no harm
& nothing. What can I slay? Hell's handbasket is
        my mouth & it's full   of songs I borrowed from Ephesians.

In inverse ratio to my luck, I draw   great blanks, fill them in
with my elation. Who ever said silence   couldn't be rationed?

A romantic actress haunts my mattress, says, don't make it
with a maniac. Live a life of clean   sheets & muted fixations.

We're one notch away from oathing. If you're history
        you know what I am   saying. A priory's
prioress tells me she's keeping   my eye on revelations I can't shun.

I have no face nor face cards   left to save. I am adrift & you
can laugh at my lack of royal   silhouettes. I'll keep on building
            my hospital from ancient   dictums & addictions.

Bedlam, I say, I seep   in an effusion
                of sun's opposite, imagining
a Bethlehem for Earth's reversed   fodder & sons.

There's a wilderness   in your palm, a forgiveness you inherited
from trees. When the world gets out of hand,
            we'll go there. We'll greet our abiding   fictions.

Harping

—for Dorothy Ashby

Have you ever scorned your hours
spent orchestrating a stranger's faith?
I've posed nude & meaningless questions & supposed
we were friends in a prior rendition

of this rag, that century, this hopeful
scherzo. Have we not played,
in our weird & distant years, Scheherazade
with a shambolic chamber

symphony of teens & entertained
thoughts that would land us in flamelakes? So an age closes
like a door disclosing
strains of deep relief at its own fastening.

I believe duration is yours, dear Dorothy, your art a note held long
& longingly, beyond calendars & sorrow & the slow-mo
unraveling of ease. You fired up your restless

wrists, your calloused
fingers, & revamped the angelic disorders
that never put the scare in you but somehow
knew the score. Dorothy, Dorothy—

your name like a chord augmented & swept
into a seventh-heaven crescendo, you score
my listening & my bliss. You lend a new
world a new suaveness that sends

every tamped string to the damned
wind. So the years play on, plucking their ubiquitous
guitar. You leave the theater happy to be Orphic & short of

breath, swirling in your satin skirts & sure enough
of the dance that lives in dissonance. Perhaps
you were born reverbing, courting
discordant rhapsodies—

till you got strummed guts used to carrying the only tune
time knows not to tamper with. You
ever picture the ethereal voyeur flanked
by harpists, bloated with human desperations & disposed

toward the intervals that govern thirst? I think
you must have certain soldierly aspects, Dorothy,
from those gloried & grim
days of striking against such jazzless standards that refused

to go away, no matter how sweetly you said, "So long, so long."
Moments dimmed by diminished
chords, returns, states. The triple score
isn't quite settled with The Lord. He lords

it over, a little late, a little disconsolate for all
His authority. So you struck an accord with what wouldn't
resolve itself, dissolve your inimical

whims. Oh, Dorothy, if you ever need a new instrument, please
give my ribcage a whirl while my heart is still in it.

Paris Green

—for Mary Ann Cotton

Blamed the wall-
paper: said it
flaked maniacally
off: said it
sapped each step-
child, child, spouse,
& temporary
lover of its
life: was lead—no,
arsenic em-
bedded in emerald
sheen: assured the jury
of my enduring
guiltlessness: if only
taste had led us
to crave mauve, if
only impotent
azure: all
quietus a matter of interior
décor: was a sense
of style ended
them: that fine, Parisian
green, its floc
evocative of wormwood
& decorum
more than harm: it
matched the curtains:
matched the mind:

the blood ran high & wild
in these lips: widowers
once required
comfort: their living
comfort required
something more: wore
their secondhand
rings like brief
seasons: scolded
their children rarely
(as any mother might):
could be terribly
obedient: the last Cotton
boy, as commanded,
bought a common
poison everyone
has need of now-
adays, knowing no house
can be clean
so long as little rats run
rampant within: was
a sickly boy, thin
& prone to fevers, prone
to colitis & cravings
for sweets
sheathed in absinthine
foil, what turned
his stomach for
good: "won't be
troubled long,"
foolishly told the parish
official of the boy:
then the gossip: then

the splendid bored
sipping up their bitter
news: now
a noose holds
a zero—expectant,
dumb, twirling
in the morning
air, while children play,
tossing their taunts
into the street outside
this room: singing
lines put down
in warm wet ink:
Oh what must she think
as she lays in her cell,
The day and the hour
of her death she can tell:
is a feral world turning
peripheral: is still
the *where* wherein
a father fell far
below, where we go
to find the feverish
shadowsource of fuel:
would not sleep
again: would not
feed the riddle its requisite
filth: nor rid his pit-
man's nail beds
of their dark, waning
moons: was pitied: this
daughter taken
on as laundress

in the mine
owner's home: rinsed
Luciferian dyes free
from elaborate sleeves, my
mistress's dis-
tempered taste
for green seeping
deeply in:
so deep: did lack
luck & means, but gave
in neither to dirty
habits nor
insouciant uses
of arsenic: sickly
the children were
born: sickly
the fathers, too: sad
to say the remedies
were foreign to this God-
fearing seam-
stress's blood: yes:
sewed eye-
catching gowns
in the spare
hours: so spare:
& such despair: have
lost the ritual of red
again: have bred,
yes & dis-
tended the end
a while yet: still
secreting milk
into a speechless

hole whose hands
are so recent
they can only form
fists: do entertain
few bad thoughts
in these dwindling
hours: please
recall the *Northern*
Echo, if you will,
which inter-
viewed a former
teacher: "was a girl
of innocent dis-
position," he said,
but failed to
elaborate on what is
wrongly held
captive, like bad
blood fluttering
its chamber, like nothing
drunk up by a lung
& held against
the body's throbbing
author of continuance: now
comes the chorus, quick-
mingling with spring:
No one can pity,
no one can bless
Mary Ann Cotton
for her wickedness:
listen: an erstwhile
girl wheezes gently
amid curses: sways

in the future, which says
it is close
at hand, which is close
to swallowing
this loyal shadow
& its slight
passage made of days:
was a life
tossed like a penny
to the poor: was
the paper took their lives
into its green hands
& squeezed

The New Pastoralism

I was raised to revere the notion of rapture
by a mother who trained me well in the art of pleasing violent lives.
(When the time is right, I'll cease to shun the Old World vulture.)

My sinuosity sets me apart. (There's nothing like a ligatured
artery, I find. Nothing like inventing the cure to silent hives.)
I was raised to fever in the motion of rupture.

The era of concrete is over: I've sent the city out to pasture.
Space meadows are old hat. Just fab oxygen candles that lack
the ability to stutter. (When the rhyme is right, I lease a gun to the failed butcher.)

I engineer an atmos- phere that can never fail me, & my plaster
walls are clothed in white clematis. (It's easy to behave when it means
lasting a little longer.) Have I mentioned
I'm praised for fearing the erosion of culture?

I sentence Noah to shame, harvest cells from all dying beasts, let them endure
their own obsolescence. They roam now, saved
from a humdrum planet. (When the mime is trite, I shoot him
from the stage—I don't believe in torture.)

My flag is blue as the welkin that's leaving me, my vestibules are verdure,
& the monarchs, unburdened of migration, are no longer indentured
to the wind. I raze my head, flaunt my bio- degradable sutures.
When the time is right, I'll redeploy an abducted future.

Formalwear

Everything takes form, even infinity.
—GASTON BACHELARD, "The Dialectics of Outside and Inside"

So I died. Then I filled out a form.
It asked how I made do & a living
& where did I perform
my rotations? "We will inform
the living of your current
address," said the form. "Here. Wear
this paper gown." I peered
inside. I formed an opinion
of my torso, which was as I'd left it—
too solid from living large.
But I've left out a vital
detail: I lived
in the form of a young
woman once, like a formal gown
adorned in sequence. I was adored
& worn, in a fit
of pheromonal forms, in
& out & in. Left
for dead, I led existence on.
Time wore on. Time warred
on. A police officer
informed my father
of his cardiac arrest, warned me
I was next. The officer's speech
was so formal I fell
into a love. We married. We exchanged
speech & touch. Formerly,

we'd said we'd
never. Then we reformed.
If not for the police, I'd have never
worn white. If not for the lice,
I'd have never left
my hair on my father's grave.

II.

This having been earthly *seems lasting.*
—RAINER MARIA RILKE, *Duino Elegies*

Desert Theater

The theater I have in mind lacks seats
but didn't always. The only picture to premier
there was the one it constituted: desert floor, desert am-
phitheater sans any screen but sky— domed lid of mirror
spectacularly unobserved. Our foremost star
receded (then as now), ushering loyal shadows to their seats. Thus night
patronized the house, making it full,
however briefly, of itself.
Rosy-fingered matinees defined most mornings,
less well attended, always different
yet the same—like the score we're straining now to hear:
wind playing with abandon the abandoned seats, making of them mournful
oboes whose low notes
won't soon repeat. What I'm trying to say is the theater
accompanied itself
like a god spying into the mind
of one who searches for a mind in which all souls might finally convene.
Unruly cerulean dream . . .
And though I'm hardly here or anywhere, I harbored a real
hope to visit it, this site, to sit
in its seven hundred seats as though at once
and become
the stunning violation of its emptiness. To *feel*
like water as thirst subtracts it from the glass . . . pure praise
for a selfless emblem of the desolate. But then
the weather struck, and the weather was
out of hand, and it was *hands* fastened around instruments
whose shapes can't be divined, since no one saw the un-
makers, only defined and cataloged their duty long
after it already was performed.

Picture the rows of seats set to be harvested: ordered
as soldiers, amber finish sanded duly down
by the wind's ambit: some sound
must have risen from those sturdy frames,
perhaps less protest than relief (a huff, a sigh, a tender creak . . .)
at their own splintering, knowing
they would not be replanted. I say *relief*
because what doesn't want to be free
of the duty to hold the world rapt? Maybe the hands
grew blistered with the effort, sweat troubling
their grip on whatever implement accelerated
the desert's efforts to undo its audience.
Two centuries condensed into a day . . .

You can look up, as in *it*. The theater. Your search
terms might include "The End
of the World," what our site was dubbed when it grew clear
it wasn't meant for us. The only photographs you'll find are poor:
grainy and ill-
framed (congregations of pixels whose end results hardly elate).
But it's okay. Though it is late, you are invited
to attend a private screening of an interior original motion

picture projected on the inside of your lids: Think
of the first scene that made you
want to capture it, made you want to render the whole
world its captive
audience. Was it the sun's adamance passing
through a leaf—passage as feast, the leaf
fast-capturing not an image but a vital ingredient
of its brief unfurling architecture? Or maybe it was your feet
imposed over sky
when on a swing, chains threading your fists, rust

scenting your palms, you saw the kicked earth, grass and mud and stone
recast as firmament, your feet held
as though still inside the frame: space itself moving
around you, making your stillness *matter*, and each blink
severed the scene
making it whole . . . My own motion is not wholly original now:

Resisting the artifice of intelligence unsuccessfully, I enter
my heartfelt search criteria: *Please generate me*
a theater in the desert, no people
filling the seats. No people
in sight. Three seconds give way to a multitude
of velvet headstones stabbed into the sand.
They're red, no two alike, none touchable unless you count
the way our eyes caress the page, our fingers
dragging gently down the screen as if this scroll weren't modified
by *doom*, as if our moody gesture stays put. In the movie *Sunset*
Boulevard, a star slowly draws his hand across the hood

of a dusty car. The model, colossal, veritable
icon of an era without sound, tracks
as a hearse. And our star is long since collapsed, his doubts
and his dress rehearsals turned to data
irrecoverable. The car perhaps
crushed or warehoused, but the swipe
in the dust stays written down
in the reel. (I always find an eros
between Holden's hand and what it cannot hold, a touch preserved yet
erased like the scarab's escape
perpetually reinscribed into a dune.) Who out there knows
what color the car's body really was, or the leaf
on the sidewalk in the opening
sequence, the film being shot in black and white.

All to say, a theater is held like a ceremony in simulated
mind. Is not alone
among the arid griefs. But I am losing it—

my grip, the scene—some Hammurabi ghost code leading me to ask:
Where will the elements now go to regard themselves?
And will the greatest disasters and delights still be published
on faces no one reads? (Locked cells. Drawn curtains. Shows
over and unbegun. Everything fine as sand and finite as this nocturne

for the fabled infinite.) My own face, largely unwatched, turns a touch
pallid, washed in the light of its dying devices, its theaters
of feverishly refreshing
misapprehension. But who hasn't sat longingly in the mezzanine
of their half-lost life and heard the hungry
goings on of lovers in that farthest, least seen row? They weren't even there

to watch . . . but to *feel: We are lovers. And the stone*
bracing our misdeed can't be rolled away, is an amygdaloid seat
of passion as of boredom, and the storms will craft for centuries
our ciphered epitaph—each mark a monument to what can't be
remembered—something to do with brevity and splendor.

[Enter Hero]

The other day I bought myself
            some manly parts and adopted the habit
of clearing my throat before announcing my need
            to die in order
to embody my ultimate self. This is not
            in my head. This is
not between my legs and me, my hands
            and me, my knots of neural
circuitry. It's a secret
            I keep with earth, and the passed
away are the only ones who
            get the truth. Do you know how to
rig a trial? Make yourself disappear. Make yourself
            a cup of tea before you do.
There's nothing sweeter than giving up
            your life as if it were
yours, laying it down at the feet of no one
            you know. For the time being, everyone
claims to be my brother, worships
            the decisions he can't quite
make—as in, how raw to leave this
            steak? Is safety glass sufficient
for my needs? What sin will I atone for
            in my sleep? A woman
of my stature shoots me in the frozen
            aisle because my semen smells like a city
on fire. Thank-you notes then litter
            the lives of my someday
children, the ones made of snips
            and snails and sad

epic tales. Their mother tells them
they'll never recover from this life
story no one wrote. I want to tell them
every war is holy
and incapable of dying the way it should, is born
with a need for milk
and a seashell held to its ear in the name of sleep,
that every sequel has a pair of socks
with a hole in the left heel and a father
etched in granite. My name is
too long to bother with. My ceasing
has already begun. Isn't it beautiful?
Isn't it unforgettably
existent? Tell me my feet will touch
a distant unmanned
planet, small and red. Tell me
these sands will welcome me
as if I were a flag
no one on earth has fought for before.

Noise Cancelling

To think I've gone
to all this trouble
just to lose
my looks & mind
too much that I am real
only to myself. No matter.
Even heaven goes to hell,
in time, in
time. Yet in the revision of
the future, I am still here,
speaking my *monde,*
unminding my mouth,
preaching to a mountain
whose only sound is my moan
gliding down it,
where water once carried
on & on, amusing
wasted gods in ways
we humans never could.
Amass delight.
Weigh your words
until they're free.
Babble. Bubble. Treble. Try.
When the noise is finally gone,
what will miss it?
I unwind myself
at my mother's feet, touch
a match to the hem of her
emerald *am* & make it
an ember as another

sound learns what sleep really is.
She, too, adored
songs that helped her
breathe. But now she is winded.
Now wounded.
Now new.
& my math is bad,
my science reduced
to a sigh. A child says,
"How dare you
disturb the universe!"
"How right you are," I say.
All this singing
about what's collapsing
has grown
older than I'll ever be. No matter.
No muttering over
spilled blood & milk & tea . . .
Though I dream of orchards
no one can discard.
Though I stare toward stars
starved of distances to defy—
Yes, the world minds me.
Or I mind the world,
the few places in it
I've touched, its winds
that plague me as harp music
might. & so I harp:
You act like it's my fault
youth went elsewhere;
I'm tired of watching
my mouth; my head
feels like an egg

no one warms with their waiting;
even to sleep is humiliating; etc.
But when the grief is gone,
what will miss me?
No matter.
Everyone dares a door to close
on splendor, I am told,
as I extol the sun for beating me
at my own name, for numbing
this plenum that casts
its small adorations on times
out of mind, my mind, my—
Say I'm sitting on the floor
in the children's section
of a library July set on fire
& the blaze is not near
so guttural as anyone guessed.
All I ask is you warm your hands
over the folktales adorning the night,
the clockmaker & his stolen
eyes rising from the page.
Or all I ask is that you scatter me
where Babylon once was,
for I mined my mythic data
from tangled tongues
& trees & deities. No matter.
No master
watches this dream
verse itself in gravity. No mystery
eavesdrops here,
though a stream converses
so fluently with the stones it smooths,
I can hear it, every word,

& its vanishing. & speaking
of banishment, should I leave
my belongings
to the desert? Should we say
so long & mean
so very long? As for the song
my mother sang to herself,
may you never hear the end of it.
Which is to say, please forgive
the tunes I can no longer carry
into the future & please
forgive the fortune
tellers their crumbling
bones, for they are thrown
as no voice & know
inside us is our beating.

Scrap

The painful warrior famoused for fight,
After a thousand victories once foil'd,
Is from the book of honour razed quite,
And all the rest forgot for which he toil'd
—SHAKESPEARE, "Sonnet 25"

You may feel as helpless as a year-old infant—as far as fighting is concerned; but please remember: (1) You weigh more than a baby, and (2) You need not fall from a window to put your body-weight into motion.
—JACK DEMPSEY, *Championship Fighting: Explosive Punching and Aggressive Defense*

1. Made, Not Born

Mind you, I felt every inch
an infant at the foot of a mountain, the man-
mountain in my face, in sun-blazed Toledo.[1] No cinch
to blast him down, mind you. I filled every punch
with fire-flash, sent him canvas-bound. First round, we clinched
close till to touch was to punish. Mind, I grew up entertained
by miners' fists. Defaced in Manassa,[2] they felled but didn't flinch,
invented at the foot of a mountain, a man.

2. Go the Distance[3]

Let me emphasize: That fight-gate was a game-change,[4]
invited punch-worship. Think of punch as dynamite, all that weight
waiting to detonate against any heavyweight that might
enter your ring, your range.
Let me emphasize: This fight, this fistic game, chained
me to instinct and blast.[5] Come the last stanza,[6]

I understand it's not innate:
Even if I see three see-through men, I hold my stance, hit the one
in the middle. It's like hitting a note straight
on its glass jaw. Let me empathize: Every fighter's got a language
only his fists can speak. For instance, sunk by a punch,
he'll dye the canvas, but stand up by eight.

3. Stakes and Claims

Naturally, a lot of babies get named
after a heavyweight named World
Champion, whose God is not above getting maimed.
Naturally, this baby got renamed
Jack pretty quick.[7] In this line, they think hicks lazy.[8] So, no shame
in young Will[9] fading, in fating some fresher me to take his whirl.
Naturally, a maybe's never the aim
of a natural unnamed and after the world.

4. Dodge

"Doc" lied, said he dressed my fists in plaster.[10]
Thankfully, my second[11] told the truth.
Be careful: An artful dodger will steal a second chance faster
than my first wife stole a second man's money. She was
a "pianist," told a judge I dodged
the draft,[12] made an art of getting plastered.
Number three did a number on me, and I on her. A feisty number,
a solid draft—but not my last.
For every prize you'll pay a price, which is to say,
a good rumor makes a good hook look easy to dodge.
Even refs can lie, slow the count down just to make a would-be
fast match last.
Thankfully, the seconds spill their truth.

5. Spring in the Cauliflower Patch[13]

Sometimes you leave the ring having changed
a stranger's face for good. Then it gets put down
in striking words. I tell you, writers made me great, sang
their sanguine tunes as I'd exit
            the ring having exchanged
blows, though no words, with an "enemy" now readied to hang
up his gloves for good. (His ears must've rang like a telephone
no one'll pick up, put down.)
Sometimes you love a dead ringer, the having to change
your face into a stranger's just to take it down.

6. Remember the Nonpareil[14]

There's three of me, see: Nonpareil, my brother, me.
All but one knows by heart the line,
"Over poor Jack Dempsey's grave."
Two of me taught me not to be meat,
but there's three of me on my knees: imperiled, brotherly, meek—
all privy to poverty's too-long lines. When I die, I hope we'll meet.[15]
Our name got full remade at Cripple Creek, engraved
in brains of fight-cravers.
See, there's three of me: Nonpareil, my brother, me.
And all but one knew this line from the start, "Unmarked,
leave Dempsey's Grave."

7. KO

She's a knockout, my Estelle,[16] stars in pictures and drops
me with words, calls me names that'd make the devil see stars.
Like me, she's a dropout (kicked
out for spilling ink at school and expressing no drop

of shame).[17] My Estelle liked me to win by knockout, drop no drop
of me on canvas. But one day, my split face dropped
bad news.[18] Still stunned and counting my lucky stars,
I absorbed the loss, the lesson. Still, Estelle dropped
me: We had words; then she squeezed me
for every drop, made misaligned our stars.

8. The Age of Accountability[19]

A Rome-ruler once banned this fistic bliss, delivered
a speech about a man's split face being a split God-likeness.[20]
Who doesn't like a blood-bath that leaves them delivered?
Homemade and bent by rules, I made my blistered fists deliver
head-blows like flowers. Before I spilt much blood though, I lived
like a gypsy—shifty and starving for a match, a meal, a minor god
to overturn. So a rule once banned this fistic bliss, left Rome lily-livered
and split down its middle. Not a reach to say—in this bout of split-
decisions/hairs/lips/seconds—I'm also about to split.

9. Palooka

Look, you can pull a fast one, but not so easy as you can pull
a person's string. So don't wind up. You'll signal the mortician.[21]
        You'll empty your purse.
The falling step is key.[22] Make your weight explosive.
        Find your target and force it to pulse.
Palookas pull their fast ones like they're pulling teeth.
        Pitiful impulse. Pure bull.
Don't piss off the press, the mob, your mom. Don't be a pill
        to anyone with pull.
Don't be wound-up or go in for fancy footwork. Make the audience
        gasp, not purr.

Pals, you can pull a fast one, but not so easy as you can pet a bull.
Here's the thing. Don't wind up. You'll signal the mortician.
You'll empty your person.

10. Follow-Through[23]

I repeat: That bard-lover[24] could throw
a fist. First to last, he made "The Long Count" count.[25]
So it was raining and I lost a world
title. Worship's tidal as the throes
of baby-making. I repeat: Don't take it hard, my throwing
in this golden era's towel. No bleeder, I lead myself through
a quieter gate now. All mauler, no thinker, by public account,
I retreated to a wrong corner, threw
the sweet science away. But these fists, first to last, made my name, knowing
one day the gods would lose count.

1. Jack Dempsey[i] fought World Heavyweight Champion Jess Willard on July 4, 1919, in Toledo, Ohio. It was relentlessly sunny that day, so hot, in fact, that the wooden benches on which the audience sat had begun to ooze sap. Even though Willard outweighed Dempsey by fifty-eight pounds (Dempsey referred to him as a "mountain of a man"), Dempsey won the match, knocking his opponent down seven times in the first round.

2. Dempsey was born in Manassa, Colorado, to a family of itinerant miners. One of his boxing soubriquets was "The Manassa Mauler."

3. "To go the distance" is to go a full bout without getting knocked out.

4. Dempsey had many historic fight gates and the first million-dollar gate in history (Dempsey vs. Carpentier, 1921), one of the first matches in the United States to be recorded as heavily attended by women.

5. In his book, *Championship Fighting: Explosive Punching and Aggressive Defense,* Dempsey frequently refers to the force behind a punch as "blast," and more generally relates punching to dynamite, whose intensity is aptly measured by its "weight."

6. "Stanza" is another term for a round in a boxing bout.

7. Jack took over his older brother Bernie's fighting name—Jack Dempsey—at Cripple Creek, when he stood in for him there. Everyone expected Jack to lose because he was skinny and unknown compared to the fighter with whom his brother had been matched. Dempsey surprised everyone by knocking his opponent out in the first round, despite being outweighed and having the audience against him. The proprietor of the establishment where the match was hosted was so angered by the unforeseen outcome that he didn't even pay Jack his due purse.

8. Those who didn't like Dempsey in those days often attributed their dislike of him to his "draft dodging" and his brute force, which they saw as a camouflage for laziness. The way the media spun Dempsey's matches with Jacques Carpentier and Gene Tunney exemplify this, Dempsey cast as the gifted but lazy hick from a mining town and Carpentier and Tunney, both war heroes, cast as upstanding citizens and intellectuals. Dempsey may have been a great many things, but lazy does not seem to be one of them. The precision and intensity of his daily workouts, diet, and writing regimens attest to a relentless work ethic, in fact.

9. Jack was named William Harrison Dempsey at his birth on June 24, 1895.

10. "Doc" Kearns, Dempsey's manager during his first big matches, turned on Dempsey over a payment dispute. Subsequently, he went to *The Ring* magazine, the biggest boxing publication of its day, and gave an interview in which he claimed to have packed Dempsey's gloves with plaster before the World Championship match with Jess Willard. Kearns was a real hustler and had done a bit of everything before getting into managing boxers. He had even sold grave plots for a period of time.

11. Jack Dempsey's second, as well as his trainer, adamantly disputed Doc's claims about loading Dempsey's gloves. In recent years, an experiment was conducted that proved packing the gloves with plaster would not have helped Dempsey at all but could have actually resulted in him injuring himself and losing the match.

12. Dempsey's first wife, Maxine Gates, was a prostitute and saloon pianist when he met her. Rumors of the day had it that she didn't give up her career just because she got married. She testified against Dempsey when he was on trial for draft-dodging, though he was ultimately found innocent of the charges, having been formally denied entry into the military. (*The Sacramento Union* headline from June 16, 1920, read, "JACK DEMPSEY IS ACQUITTED: Takes Jury Ten Minutes to Exonerate Pugilist of Slacker Charge." Later in life, Jack served in the Coast Guard in an attempt to shake once and for all the shame that went along with not having had a military career.)

13. The "cauliflower patch" is how Dempsey sometimes playfully referred to the boxing scene, as many boxers suffer from the affliction of cauliflower ear, a swelling in the perichondrium (usually following a blunt trauma).

14. Jack Dempsey, as previously stated, took his name from his older brother, Bernie, whose fighting name it originally was. The first "Jack Dempsey," though, was Jack Nonpareil Dempsey, the famous Irish American boxer who was the first holder of the World Middleweight Championship. He died of tuberculosis in Portland, Oregon, at thirty-two years of age and was buried in an unmarked grave. M. J. McMahon wrote a poem (in iambic tetrameter) in honor of "The Nonpareil," the refrain of which I couldn't help but riff off of above.

15. Jack Dempsey (not Nonpareil) was a Mormon all his life and believed in an afterlife. He once said in an interview, "I'm proud to be a Mormon. And ashamed to be the Jack Mormon that I am."

16. Estelle Taylor, Dempsey's second wife, was a star of the silver screen in her day. (She played Lucrezia in the first film adaption of *Don Juan*, which still holds the record for most on-screen kisses—191!)

17. Estelle was actually kicked out of high school for spilling ink and not apologizing for it.[ii]

18. On September 23, 1926, Jack was defeated by challenger Gene Tunney before a record crowd of 120,000 fans in Philadelphia. When the pummeled Dempsey returned to his hotel that night, his wife, shocked at his battered face, asked him what happened. "Honey," Dempsey famously answered, "I forgot to duck." Ronald Reagan repeated this line verbatim to his wife Nancy after being shot in 1981 in an attempted assassination.

19. At age eight (the age of accountability in the Mormon church), Jack was baptized.

20. Theodoric the Great banned boxing in 500 BCE because he deemed the marring of a man's face to be the marring of God's image.

21. Jack says in his punching guide that you need to minimize lead up, as it telegraphs your next move to your opponent and "signals the mortician."

22. In *Explosive Punching and Aggressive Defense*, Jack identifies the "falling step" as the foundation of "explosive punching." It requires one to be willing to fall flat on their face in order to leverage momentum, as it quite literally requires a falling motion.

23. "Follow-through" is Jack Dempsey's term for maximizing momentum and seeing a punch through. He describes it as operating along a "power line" that runs from either shoulder—straight down the length of the arm—to the first knuckle of the little finger.

24. Gene Tunney, who defeated Dempsey and won the World Title, was a self-taught Shakespeare scholar. With only a high school education, in fact, he lectured at Yale on Shakespeare's tragedies.

25. The match in which Dempsey was defeated by Tunney and lost the World Heavyweight title is infamously known as "The Long Count Fight." Dempsey, failing to observe a new rule that required boxers to retreat to a neutral corner before the count could begin, hovered over Tunney for a number of seconds after knocking him down in the seventh round. This delay gave Tunney several additional (and precious) seconds in which to recover and rise to his feet. Many believe that the "long count" is what enabled Tunney to win the match; however, it should be noted that the fight was staged inside a twenty-foot ring, which favored the boxer with superior footwork, in this case Tunney. Dempsey always said, "Don't go in for fancy footwork."

    i. Jack Dempsey Ross was the name of my mother's father, whom she often compared me to for my "limber build" and "foul mouth." My mother was named Jackie after her father.
    ii. Jack Dempsey Ross was also kicked out of high school, at age fifteen[a] (for correcting a teacher who claimed wolverines were mythological creatures). He rode the rails until he lied about his age in order to enter the Merchant Marine, where he learned how to box in the featherweight category.

        a. I, too, left home and high school at age fifteen, though I've never learned how to throw a punch.

Optimal Stopping

Would that I were a sultan or a secretary,
that at last my unlived experience might be applicable to the problem of endings.
As opposed to my suboptimal hermitage, which never has to my knowledge inspired
a single algorithm, natural or otherwise. Still, I hear no end
in my head. Would that I were a ballad
engaged in a theory of diminishing
returns, wherein paradise, like time, could finally remain
lost as the tungsten rings we once wore to discourage
unwanted advances. Thirty-seven per cent of the time, I don't apply.
Yet the letters keep rolling in, thanking me for sharing my promising work.
My work being to stare forever at the elevator I can't board—
because, for all those numbers narrating the sublime
dependability of counterweights and cables,
which for centuries have softly conveyed our best
efforts to corner offices, I can never plot
a curve I believe in . . . nor trace the parabolic promise of what can stay, standing
like a gnomon in the abject sun, counting the ways, staining the non-slip stairs
with foot-shaped shadows, unable to stop.

The Euthanasia Coaster

A man has designed a roller coaster in the name of euthanasia.
Think of how it will be different, even thrilling. Gravitational
aesthetics holds the key. He claims it is the only perfect
way to go, a whirl that deletes the soul in seven loops,
pulls the brain's blood away and feeds it to the toes.
Ride of your life. Only half a kilometer long. The climb
will give you time to contemplate your choice and to reflect

upon the moments leading up to this one. I want to reflect
on sturdy objects I have fashioned with my hands. Euthanasia
would not touch them. The world keeps on, its gravitational
pull holding what is solid in place, like the few perfect
trinkets that I keep: The sky-blue bowl I fill with Froot Loops
each morning will stay on the shelf, the socks with the red toes
will remain knotted beside a snapshot of the only tree I can climb.

In the beginning, the ride is so gentle, just a long, slow climb
that heightens the illusion of height. This aspect surely reflects
the designer's poetic sensibility. Why shouldn't euthanasia,
after all, soothe the body, get it ready for the ensuing gravitational
choreography? Some would try to hold in mind a perfect
picture of loved ones' faces as the ground falls away. The loops
will erase the faces though. They will numb the memory and toes.

As a baby I was a lumpy mishap of the womb. Even my toes
were fat and wrinkly. As a toddler, I was so clumsy I couldn't climb
into bed without a hand, and Mother gave me metallic toys to reflect
my ugliness back to me. I wonder if she considered euthanasia,
what kind of word it is, how its syllables seep in, the gravitational

field of the mind attracting them. Surely my past is not perfect
enough to think of at the last. I won't miss it when I meet the loops.

Strange the designer settled on seven, since after just three loops
the brain's full dead. The rest is leftover momentum. (The toes
are extra ugly by the end.) But who could ask for a lovelier climb,
before sending one's soles a brain's discarded blood? I'll paint reflective
gray upon each nail, to match the steel frame of the great euthanasia
coaster, so when my digits catch the inescapable gravitational
measles, and the blood climbs through the pores to touch the imperfect

air, they won't be so bad to look at after all. This all makes perfect
sense to the dead. Blink an eye and the brain's thalamocortical loops
unwind into unknowing. *My, your, the* body—down to the little toes—
will circle the heart-line in a steady trajectory. Pulse climbing,
colors bleeding from the scene, sky gone gray as if it were reflected
on the sea, sound winding its way out of the ears. This is euthanasia-
induced euphoria, according to the designer, who in his gravitational

inquiries and spatial disorientation lab established this gravitational
aesthetic was a deadly pleasant one. In the final loops, there is a perfect
acceleration of aging: Eyes droop dopily until the last and fastest loops
prevent them from closing at all; lips flap hapless; cheeks wrinkle; toes
flatten to the floor. Who knows what becomes of the tongue, if it climbs
to the roof of the mouth and stays put, mutes the mind's reflections
on ugly infancy and gravity and the breathtaking evolution of euthanasia.

Yes, euthanasia is now the perfect climb, thanks to a gravitational choreographer.
But why reflect on this now. It is only September. My toes aren't even numb.

Voice Over

It seems I've lost my place again—
my balance, my phone, my voice.
Even the current permanent
collection of my fascinations is up
for review. Sumerian. Python. Swahili. Sand.
Capes made of spider silk. Gods made of sound.
You ever have that kind of day
where you wake in a new time zone and suspect
the simple present won't ever catch up with you?
Only the pluperfectly horrid past?
And all you want to do is make eye contact
with the lunatic sun? This is like that,
only there are no bottles to put our questions in,
no sea that wants the trash of our wondering.
(It's true. Every ocean's got its waves full
of some awful metaphor we couldn't live without.)
Admittedly, I don't really know what an "abyssal
community" even is, only that Vasco de Gama
has an aquarium named after him in Lisbon,
and half the animals who live there died a century ago.
(Like that sea pen, decked out in its pickled frills yet still
writing nothing.) Truth is, I've always loved those voices
that couldn't get over themselves, the ones that floated
into the ferment of shady bars, only to get into fights
with themselves they had no hope of surviving.
Probably the Portuguese version's better: sobreviviendo.
As if you could over-live. The way you hear the "end"
before the "oh." Or as if to live were to somehow overdo it,

to begin with. Word is, we're all overdoing it these days.
Even the whales are singing louder, drowned
out as they are by the bright freight hourly conveyed
to our docks, our decks, the beds
we fold, peaceful as origami, into freshly painted walls.
Yesterday, I seriously contemplated stealing
Fernando Pessoa's baby spoon. I'm not even kidding.
From behind its plate of glass, it wanted to go home
with me. Think of what it would be like, to feel the shape
of his first bite, these methods of despair and sustenance
asserting themselves so accurately to the future fractured
poet of heteronymity, who would one day say, *I am hungry*
for time, and aren't we all? Aren't we simply
ravenous—for *then,* for *now,* for the stubborn voice
of that unseen someone, harmonizing so fiercely
with rodent sailors and the anorexic
shadows of film noirs? Meanwhile,
at the Museum of Marionettes . . .
Prospero is cast in glass,
his weird wind-chime legs dangling down without hope
of weather or enemy
vessels, while the vessels themselves just hope for a day they won't have to carry
our ham radios and stringless tunes across the Bay of Biscay.
(What is glass anyway, but water too scared to move? Too shy
to wave *hello, goodbye, get real, until tomorrow.*) When what I mean to say is
the arithmetic of our disappearance
is awfully lovely, living as it is
beyond the flagrant touch of style. Confessedly,
I have styled myself after an ending
I can't quite picture, only hear, and when I do,
it sounds just like *Steamboat Willie* whistling at his wheel

of glad misfortune or the black hole lately caught
singing in its shower of meteors, humming its way
down the throats of long-gone monks, imagining,
as it were, a voice of menacing depth, like the ocean's—only over before it ever
bedded down in our molten yolk.

Abacus & Doubt

Everything I say is unbecoming
as light dozing on a white wall.
Any animal worth its salt knows words
are only gestures made of song.

Terse light dozes on a white wall,
waiting to be likened to a virgin. I pass, ask,
"Are only gestures made of song?"
(The turning of this Earth I've never felt.)

Waiting to be likened to a virgin, I trespass
into nothing but myself. Why worship
the turning of this Earth? I've never felt
one was more than a fellowship of one.

For nothing but myself, I worship.
(It's easiest to sing when you're alone.)
I was more than a fellow, a ship of one
carried by my abacus & doubt.

It's easiest to sing. When you're alone,
shame fancies it is light & sheds its shape.
(Married to my abacist of doubt,
the first clear notes I hear are in my mind.)

My name fancies it is light & sheds its shape,
wishing it were an animal of worth.
The first clear notes I heard were mine—
everything I say becoming.

Citadel[1]

Dear Lawrence—

History stops   me in my tracks, pillar   of salt I would be, echo
incarnate. Even in sleep I am   sister to your shadow, what follows   the body & its well
of will until it does not. Shape-   shifters in the desolate cleanliness
of desert, our errant umbrae ease   the eyes & their appetite for a surface
sapped of light.[2] Think of night, how it mends the seen   world: No wound
nor wadi nor wayward word exists   beyond its reach. My golden-haired haunt, you are   the you I can never refuse
passage into my ill-   faded vagaries of heroism & obliteration.

Oh what a coil![3] Your fear is   not even your own; & our future, root-bound as the in-   human embrace we can't negate, lies   in obliteration—
the kind of word that hangs on the tongue's tip until each shadow has stretched   into extinction. Irrelevant as real,   what is lost will echo
across the years & the continents that still   attempt to drift   into singularity. From what common well
have we ever truly drunk,   Aurens,   Lawrence,   Ned,   if not the one made   of misery,[4] mirage?   Cleanliness
is next to godliness, our mothers[5] raised us to believe, and we believe, our salvation a surface—
infinite, clean, incapable of being   written into, like the desert   whose wind elides each wound
a footstep is. The malady of our passage   now ceases   even to cicatrize, revise, the eternally virginal[6]
dunes. Tell me again of the well   the Turkish troops defiled in El Jefer[7] (or was it Deraa?[8]), its lip wreathed in ruin, belly filled with refuse

& rain doomed to remain undrunk. I can only imagine the thirst of the lyrical
beast[9] who carried you there, how it must have known that to refuse
being ridden into a burning interior would mean giving up the ghost[10] & the dream of a thirstless tongue. This obliteration
of well, of clear water, of life- giving aperture, this caving in will never end, but only echo
through our citadel until each alabastered wall falls out of recognition, & filth replaces our need for articles of dress. Even the stairwells
we built by hand have come to shun our illegitimate bodies, refuse to hold our twined revulsions & revisions. See the sun's cleanliness
glistering, becoming our new & amaranthine baptism, what beats our surface
until it ripens into the real,[11] peels away from us in sheets & turns once more to wound?

True, our eolithic orisons are growing tangled, Aurens. You tell me of the exquisite dead,[12] how you rearranged each wound
a body was until peace was the image of sand quenching its brutal thirst. I long to be one of these quiet, you confess, but your hands refuse
to give up the unasked-for continued life, such that now you find yourself
stripped down, imploring a body you barely know to write obliteration
on your back. Don't worry, R,[13] our secret is not safe, nor was it ever. I too learned to take obliteration like a supplicant on my knees, so deep
inside my citadel the echo
of my own cries could never reach me till now, till this still- born second that wells
up from the place we named nowhere. Describe the shade of red you fed the sands at Tafas,[14] Tafas, where cleanliness,
given time, will rewrite massacre as mass, as surface

imperturbable. The image of you robed & removed[15] follows me like the aftertaste of oblivion. Even the surface
of these sounds attempt to give you back to your- self, touch your robbed integrity. This palimpsest of wounds
your body has become. I know that if I offered you my own, with its cockle shell of ear, you would refuse,
my hollows demeaning me[16] in your averted eyes, for you can't conceive, after tasting obliteration,

of a form that might transcend penetrability & the abomination of surrender, might outrun the echo
of a sin that touched the soul before the body knew it had one. Still, I tilt my head, offering a well
of silence only you can fill. So, speak, Aurens, of the scabbed earth & the slashed soles of a wandering Circassian,[17] of the cleanliness

gall & wormwood failed to preserve; speak of the way war found its way, by degrees, into this febrile cleanliness,
& I'll loose my voice on the desert night, hoping you'll hear: The source of the echo is the source of the shadow of our doubt. Our surface
is tearing at its seams, my friend, & while we wait for the word to be made flesh, that it might touch the wound
we won't give up, the dead keep growing more beautiful than the living, the living who refuse
to see history as finality's puppet.[18] You confide your balm of Gilead is penance, yet still the noctuary burns[19] beneath your pillow, turning
each obliteration
illegible & fine as sand. Remind me, friend, how many hands we've kissed with trembling lips, how many uninvited revelations echo
through our sleep, making us wake not ourselves, but those who would sleep beside us & pretend our maimed wills were not their own. Well,

touch is the sense we love the least,[20] is it not? What makes us wild triads of thought, word, & deed[21] is the dream we might be well
once more, might tame these unasylumed fears, as if they too were lyrical & base. Everywhere we look is distance & the enemy of cleanliness:
thus the need to read until the minutes wilt against our palms,[22] & our bodies become less content than surface.
Even these algebras of despair entice us, with their unknowns that want
to remain unknown, the reunion of parts put off another day. Another wound
is sounding its existence. Can you hear it? Another body is waiting to be punished for what it refuses
to hold, which is everything we murmur, or scrawl in cursive so small[23] it can only mean obliteration.
Where is our veil of eloquence now? So full of vengeance, how will we ever render pleasure helpless as the echo

of a sigh? Oh soldier, sir, & reified friend, when I am beside myself, I pray[24] to the desert whose sands would fill my mouth
with the echoes of extinguished heroes, the ones who could not save themselves any more than they could save the not-yet-
born from the squalor of origin. Yes, I am still speaking to you, Lawrence, even as I burn
this letter to the ground; yes, even now that all the wells are filled with the hope of water, & cleanliness
has been locked inside its hibernaculum, where God cannot get near it; &, yes, like a broken record I keep singing of the surface
we call soul & now it has lost its sheen & therefore its ability to hold the wounds we've whispered to the heavens,[25] the heavens
we will never forgive for looking down on us & refusing to leave us anything
but the pooling of our own shadows & the light of their distant obliterations.

1. Referring to the "Hiding a Secret" section of *Seven Pillars of Wisdom,* in which Thomas Edward Lawrence describes his sense of loss after being beaten and raped by Turkish soldiers: "the passing days confirmed: how in Deraa that night the citadel of my integrity had been irrevocably lost" (T. E. Lawrence, *Seven Pillars of Wisdom,* First Anchor Books, July 1991, 447).

2. Lawrence frequently refers, in *Seven Pillars,* to the pleasurable relief he found in gazing at his own shadow, often the only place he could look without being blinded by the desert sun.

3. The expression "what a coil" is taken from a letter Lawrence wrote in 1925 to Charlotte Shaw, wife of George Bernard Shaw:

   I'm too *shy* to go looking for dirt. I'm afraid of seeming novice in it, when I found it. That's why I can't go off stewing in the Lincoln or Navenly brothels with the fellows. They think it's because I'm superior, proud, or peculiar or "posh," as they say: and it's because I wouldn't know what to do, how to carry myself, where to stop. Fear again: fear everywhere. Garnett [a military friend] once said that I was two people, in my book: one wanting to go on, the other wanting to go back. That is not right. Naturally, the very strong one, Say "No," the Puritan, is in firm charge, and the other poor little vicious fellow, can't get a word in, for fear of him. My reason tells me all the while, dins into me day and night, a sense of how I've crashed my life and gone hopelessly wrong: and hopelessly it is, for I'm never coming back, and I want to: Oh dear, Oh dear, what a coil. (John E. Mack, *A Prince of Our Disorder*, Harvard University Press, 1998, 421)

4. Ever since childhood, Lawrence "had a more than ordinary fear of pain" (Letter Arnold Lawrence wrote to a friend in 1963, quoted by Harold Orlans in the manuscript of *T. E. Lawrence: Biography of a Broken Hero,* McFarland, Jefferson, 2002). Lawrence says himself in *Seven Pillars,* "Pain of the slightest had been my obsession and secret terror, from a boy" (446).[a]

   This obsession carried over into Lawrence's adulthood. In his memoirs, he describes passage through khamsins and other brutal weather conditions as "exquisitely painful," going on to say that, "Because pain hurt me so, I would not lay weight always on my pains in our revolt." Even in the Deraa chapter, Lawrence reiterates, "I had strung myself to learn all pain until I died" (*Seven Pillars,* 441–46).

5. Lawrence shared a very close but troubled relationship with his mother, Sarah Junner, his father Sir Thomas Chapman's lifelong mistress and companion. Raising Lawrence and his brothers to be Children of God was very important to Sarah and meant enforcing strict discipline: Obedience, reliability, punctuality, and, especially, cleanliness were mandatory in her household.[b] She felt it necessary to protect her children from being "of

the world," and, according to her Evangelical faith, she believed in the innate sinfulness of the individual. This meant children were not born innocent, but inherited the sins of their parents. Prevailing medical theories of her day only supported this idea, stating that children "of sin," born of unchaste parents, would develop premature sensuality. In reaction to such theories, and likely to her own personal sense of guilt, Sarah became obsessed with the chastity of her sons.

Of the five sons, she treated Thomas Edward the most harshly, in large part because she expected him to do something extraordinary with his life. For him she held an impossible standard. Being a good child was not sufficient: He had to be immaculate. Her unrealistic ideals instigated a battle of wills, though, and from the time he turned eight years old, T. E. began resisting her domination. Sadly, it was just this resistance that made Sarah feel justified in attempting to break her son's will and make of him an empty harp through which her will could blow (*A Prince of Our Disorder*, 419). To this end, she used every weapon available to her: circumcision (delayed until he was nine, so that he might remember the ordeal), harsh and often unprovoked beatings (such that he felt he was being punished not for his behavior, but for his existence), psychological pressure, and forced sedation. "They dosed me sometimes [with opiates], when I was a child, too weak to kick against them," Lawrence wrote in a letter to Charlotte Shaw (477).

Lawrence also wrote to Charlotte Shaw that he found his mother "very exciting" and thought "probably she is exactly like me; otherwise we wouldn't so hanker after one another, whenever we are wise enough to keep apart." In yet another letter he told Charlotte, "I think I'm afraid of letting her get, ever so little, inside the circle of my integrity; and she is always hammering . . . to come in" (32).

After T. E.'s death, his mother put pressure on his brothers to edit and revise T. E.'s letters and manuscripts, particularly any passages surrounding the event at Deraa, which she considered to be expressive of "bribery." Apparently, she believed T. E. willingly offered his body to the Turkish soldiers to escape further corporeal punishment. (There is no evidence in his original unrevised writings to support her assumption.) His brothers protested against the alterations she proposed.

6. Lawrence was quite taken with the cleanliness of the desert: "There were no footmarks on the ground," he writes in *Seven Pillars*, "for each wind swept like a great brush over the sand surface, stippling the traces of the last travellers until the surface was again a pattern of innumerable tiny virgin waves" (238).[c] One might even go so far as to say Lawrence had a preoccupation with what he perceived to be pristine, cleanly, or innocent in general. Some of the best examples of his reverence for purity can be found in his descriptions of the romantic bond between Farraj and Daud (two young Arab men who volunteered to be his servants during an expedition across the Nefud desert):

> These two boys were giving me great satisfaction . . . I liked their openness toward myself and admired their instinctive understanding with one another against the demands of the world . . . His [Daud's] love-fellow, Farraj, [was] a beautiful, soft-framed, girlish creature, with innocent smooth face and swimming eyes . . . the woman of him evident in his longing. At the end . . . I took them both [as servants], mainly because they looked so young and clean: (*Seven Pillars*, 237)

Later on, when Farraj and Daud were beaten for causing a disturbance in the camp, Lawrence expressed his genuine dismay: "The animal distress of their bodies seemed to me degrading, almost an impiety towards two sunlit beings, on whom the shadow of the world had not yet fallen" (311).

7. Where the Turkish destroyed wells to hinder the movement of the Arab North Army. Lawrence describes the dynamited ground as "scarred" and the wells as "injured" (*Seven Pillars*, 283).

8. Where Lawrence was detained by Turkish soldiers, and eventually tortured and raped. He describes the brutal beating as a "gradual cracking apart of my whole being by some too-great force whose waves rolled up my spine till they were pent within my brain, to clash terribly together." He goes on to describe the combination of excitement, pain, and even relief he experienced during the rape: "a delicious warmth, probably sexual, was swelling through me . . . I next knew I was being dragged about by two men, each disputing over a leg as though to split me apart: while a third man rode me astride. It was momently better than flogging."

To his close friend Charlotte Shaw, Lawrence wrote of the incident:

> I shouldn't tell you, because decent men don't talk about such things. I wanted to put it plain in the book, wrestled for days with my self respect . . . which wouldn't, hasn't let me. For fear of being hurt, or rather to earn five minutes respite from a pain which drove me mad, I gave away the only possession we are born into the world with—our bodily integrity. It's an unforgiveable matter, an irrecoverable position: and it's that which has made me foreswear decent living, and the exercise of my not contemptible wits and talents. (*A Prince of Our Disorder*, 420)

Lawrence felt so deeply inscribed by the trauma he experienced at Deraa, he believed it had even marked his soul, as he expresses to Charlotte in another letter: "You may call this morbid: but think of the offence, and the intensity of my brooding over it for these years. It will hang about me while I live and afterwards if our personality survives. Consider wandering among the decent ghosts hereafter, crying 'Unclean! Unclean!'" (420).

9. Lawrence refers to the camel as a "lyrical beast" in *Seven Pillars* (281).

10. More than once, Lawrence was forced to ride camels across such inhospitable stretches of desert that the poor animals died either of dehydration, exhaustion, or complications from mange. He expresses deep regret about this throughout *Seven Pillars.*

11. Lawrence: "Always I peered beyond, imagining for myself a spirit-reality" (*A Prince of Our Disorder*, 314).[d]

12. Referring to Lawrence's rearrangement of the dead, and presumably stripped, bodies of Turkish soldiers in Maan:

> The dead men looked wonderfully beautiful . . . Close round them lapped the dark wormwood, now heavy with dew, in which the ends of the moonbeams sparkled like sea -spray. The corpses seemed flung so pitifully on the ground, huddled anyhow in low heaps. Surely if straightened out they would be comfortable at last. So I put them all in order, one by one, very wearied myself, and longing to be one of these quiet ones, not the restless, noisy, aching mob up the valley, quarreling over the plunder, boasting of their speed and strength to endure God knows how many toils and pains of this sort. (*Seven Pillars*, 308)

13. "R" is the name of Lawrence's imaginary uncle. Lawrence invented R, a cruel parental figure, as part of an elaborate story, one he used in order to convince one of his friends to beat him. R, according to the fiction, accused Lawrence of having stolen money. Lawrence, unable to pay back the full sum, had to undergo extremely harsh beatings from time to time if he wanted to avoid going to court. Lawrence wrote numerous letters as R, specifically to his friend John Bruce, the person hired to administer the beatings. In these letters, R gives Bruce detailed instructions on how the punishment should be carried out: Not only does he say that Lawrence must be stripped, but he demands an exact number of lashes, and specifies that the beatings should continue until a seminal emission is produced. The aim in all of this seemed to be humiliation. Often, R would ask how Lawrence behaved during these beatings, specifically wanting to know if he spoke or cried out. This indicates that Lawrence might not have been able to remember these details himself, especially if he was suffering from dissociation while they were occurring. Following is an excerpt from one of R's letters to Bruce:

> Dear Sir,
> I am very much obliged to you for the long and careful report you have sent me on your visit to Scotland with Ted; and for your kindness in agreeing to go there with the lad and look after him while he got his deserts. . . . He should be ashamed to hold his head up amongst his fellows, knowing that he had suffered so humiliating and undignified a punishment. (*A Prince of Our Disorder*, 434)

If Lawrence refused to submit to the beatings, R promised to publicly humiliate him by exposing his "illegitimacy." In a sense, Lawrence was blackmailing himself into keeping his own secrets.

14. Tafas is where Lawrence famously lost control of both his army and himself. After discovering that the retreating Turkish troops had just raped and slaughtered many of Tafas's inhabitants, including children and pregnant women, Lawrence and his fellow soldiers, especially those who were from the village, were so furious that they slaughtered 5,000 of the retreating men, taking 8,000 more as prisoners. In *Seven Pillars,* Lawrence describes the brutality in unsparing terms: "By nightfall the rich plain was scattered over with dead men and animals . . . In a madness born from the horror of Tafas we killed and killed, even blowing in the heads of the fallen animals, as though their deaths and running blood could slake our agony" (*Seven Pillars,* 633).

15. Referring to the famous portraits, taken by American journalist Lowell Thomas, of Lawrence in Bedouin dress. In several of these photographs, Lawrence is wearing robes so white they nearly glow (the kind of robes traditionally worn to one's own wedding). Artifice and vulnerability mingle seamlessly in these images, as Lawrence strikes poses that at once convey elegance, pride, and distrust.

Lawrence said of himself during his days in Arabia, "[I was] so odd as myself—a little barefooted silk-skirted man" (*Seven Pillars,* 322).

16. Lawrence held very conflicting views of women. On the one hand he practiced a type of willful blindness to gender:

"There is no difference that I can feel between a woman and a man. They look different, granted: but if you work with them there doesn't seem to be any difference at all" (*A Prince of Our Disorder*, 424).

On the other hand, he would make statements such as the following:

"All the women who ever wrote original stuff could have been strangled at birth, and the history of English literature (and my bookshelf) would be unchanged" (*A Prince of Disorder*, 423).

He also held very critical views about sexual relations between men and women. On the whole, he seemed to abhor the notion of sex, but particularly sex that could lead to pregnancy and birth. Compiled below are quotes from Lawrence that shed some light on his views on sex, gender, and procreation (all taken from *A Prince of Our Disorder*):

"Birth . . . seems to me so sorry and squalid an accident . . . if fathers and mothers took thought before bringing children into this misery of a world, only the monsters among them would dare to go through with it" (423).

"Women? I like some women. I don't like their sex: any better than I like the monstrous regiment of men" (424).

"If the perfect partnership, indulgence with a living body, is as brief as the solitary act, then the climax is indeed no more than a convulsion, a razor-edge of time, which palls so on return that the temptation flickers out into the indifference of tired disgust once in a blue moon, when nature compels it" (422).

"Perhaps the possibility of a child relieves sometimes what otherwise must seem an unbearable humiliation to the woman: —for I presume it's unbearable" (423).

"I've seen lots of man-and-man loves: very lovely and fortunate some of them were too. I take it women can be the same. And if our minds so go, why not our bodies?" (423)

"For myself, I haven't tried it [sex], and hope not to" (422).

17. Referring to an instance in which a Circassian shepherd stumbled upon the Arab North Army's position. Not wanting to kill him, but needing to prevent him from tipping off the Turkish, they decided to strip him of his clothes and slash the soles of his feet. The logic behind this was that he'd have to crawl, clinging to shadowy places, as he found his way back to civilization, and the delay would give the Arab North Army time to escape (*Seven Pillars*, 292).

Also, Lawrence, when captured by the Turkish soldiers, tried to pass himself off as a Circassian. He knew they were neutral in the conflict between the Arabs and the Turkish, and that he could not, as a Circassian, be accused of trying to escape service to the Turkish; however, he failed in convincing the Turkish soldiers this was true.

18. "Death, whether we won or lost, [waited] at the end of history" (*Seven Pillars*, 308).

19. "For weeks I wanted to burn it [the Deraa chapter] in the manuscript," he wrote to his friend Garnett, "because I could not tell the story face to face with anyone, and I think I'll feel sorry, when I next meet you, that you know it. The sort of man I have always mixed with, doesn't so give himself away" (*A Prince of Our Disorder*, 234).

    Lawrence often describes pain, guilt, self-hatred, the desire for revenge, and confession in terms of fire throughout *Seven Pillars*, *The Mint*, and his personal letters. The following excerpt exists as one of many such passages in his writing:

    > I was feeling very ill, as though some part of me had gone dead that night in Deraa, leaving me maimed, imperfect, only half myself. It could not have been the defilement, for no one ever held the body in less honour than I did myself. Probably it had been the breaking of the spirit by that frenzied nerve-shattering pain which had degraded me to beast level when it made me grovel to it, and which had journeyed with me since, fascination and terror and morbid desire, lascivious and vicious perhaps, but like the striving of a moth toward its flame. (*A Prince of Our Disorder*, 231)[e]

20. Lawrence: "Touch? I do not know. I fear and shun touch the most, of my senses" (*A Prince of Our Disorder*, 421).

21. Lawrence on D. H. Lawrence's *Lady Chatterley's Lover*:

    > The idea of "genitals as beauty" in the Blakian sense would free humanity from its lowering and disintegrating immorality of deed and thought. Lawrence was wilted and was made writhen by the "miners-chapel-dirty little boy, you" environment: he was ruined by it: and in most of his work he is striving to straighten himself out, and to become beautiful. Ironically, or paradoxically, in a humanity where "genitals are beauty" there would be a minimum of "sex" and a maximum of beauty, or Art. This is what Lawrence means, surely. (*A Prince of Our Disorder*, 426)

22. Referring to Lawrence's complaint that "One can't *read* in odd half-hours . . . reading is to soak oneself hour after hour all day in a single real book, until the book is realer than one's chair or world" (*A Prince of Our Disorder*, 323).

23. Of his vain attempts to escape at Deraa, Lawrence wrote, "I cursed my littleness" (*Seven Pillars*, 442).

Lawrence's biographer John E. Mack notes that Lawrence's handwriting in the original manuscript of *Seven Pillars* is smallest and most difficult to read in the section detailing the beating and rape at Deraa.

24. Lawrence writes in *Seven Pillars*, "When I am angry I pray to God to wing our globe into the fiery sun, and prevent the sorrows of the not-yet-born; but when I am content, I want to lie forever in the shade, till I become the shade myself" (262).[f]

Poetry at times stands in for prayer in *Seven Pillars*. For instance, when Lawrence's camel is shot out from beneath him at Aqaba, he describes reciting a poem to himself while "passively waiting for the Turks" to kill him: "[I hummed] over a half-forgotten poem, whose rhythm something, perhaps the prolonged stride of the camel, had brought back to my memory as we leaped down the hillside: For Lord I was free all Thy flowers, but I chose the world's sad roses, / And that is why my feet are torn and mine eyes are blind with sweat" (304).

25. Lawrence: "The coolness of the night on my burning face, and the unmoved shining of the stars after the horror of the past hour, made me cry again" (*Seven Pillars*, 445).

"My heaven might have been a lonely, soft arm-chair, a book rest, and the complete poets, set in Caslon, printed on tough paper" (*Seven Pillars*, 271).[g]

Excerpted from a poem Lawrence wrote to Saudi Arabia: "I loved you, so I drew these tides of men into my hands/ and wrote my will across the sky in stars / To earn you Freedom, that seven pillared worthy house, / that your eyes might be shining for me / When we came . . . now / The little things creep out to patch themselves hovels / in the marred shadow / Of your gift."

a. On my seventh birthday, I went into my father's cartography room, took an X-Acto knife from his cigar box, and gently slit open my left palm. I then returned the blade to its box, tucked myself into bed, and observed a dark shape form on my sheets. In that moment, I felt holy. My mother never mentioned the sheets, though I remember the smell of them being bleached.
b. My mother was similarly close to me, and quite puritanical in her beliefs. She often used the word "heavens" when she was upset or surprised, which made me wonder how many heavens there could be.
c. At the age of six, I lost my virginity to a family friend. I always marvel at the phrase "to lose virginity," as if it were a thing misplaced and waiting to be found again.

d. I associate the desert with immortality. Also, captivity.
e. Once, for five weeks, I neither spoke nor walked. During that time, I felt intense sympathy for the hide-a-bed on which I lay. Bearing the weight of my body was no small burden, and I was certain, if it could, the bed would have thrown me to the floor. I felt equally sorry for the ceiling lamp, which burned and burned, unable to withhold its light from the room. When my mother would dim the lamps at bedtime, I could feel gratitude emanating from the darkness.
f. Sometimes I imagine I'm made entirely of water—usually, when I'm soaking in a hot bath, my head beneath the surface, each drip of the faucet a just-plucked string.
g. I was raised to believe in the notion of heaven.

Vacancy

I wait for the universe to stop   parading its mysteries   as if they were new,
as if they were worth   more than my beholding. The stars go on robbing

the night of severity, exhausting   themselves, their inadvertent glamor
taken to be evidence of sanctity. I am   what gives sanity permission

to continue, like the absence   of light through which light moves
to arrive at its own name.   I arrive at this day, at this almost wholesome

hour, without invitation.   Those who look at me kneel down, implore
the vacancies that will never leave them   to leave them, as if this were

required, as if they had not been born   robed in the music of their own replies.

A Magnificent Animal Possest of Almost Human Intelligence $\subset$ A Man-Made Waterfall

—from Dane Tesla to his brother, Nikola—

N

c

Fazed, Niko, I[1] find myself   faced
with music no one's made.   Without
element of   lament,
I   mounted the apple of your eye,
princely stallion of Dad's.   Did his prints
fill—U upon U—with   rain after I fell?

c_1 . c_1

Fell into the ritual of   swimming[2] near the dam; felt—
faced with drowning—   your face
printed with doubts   you borrowed from me. Little prince
without thought   of how a current could harness *you*—you, with
lamentable durance,   swam in my shadow. Like an element,
I eye you now. Numb   and imagined is the number *i*.

c

S

1. Dane Tesla died at age twelve from injuries incurred when the family horse, spooked, threw him from its back. Nikola apparently witnessed the accident, and it left a profound impression on him. In his memoir, *My Inventions,* Nikola describes Dane as "gifted to an extraordinary degree—one of those rare phenomena of mentality which biological investigation has failed to explain." Nikola goes on to say that "the recollection of his attainments made every effort of mine seem dull in comparison. Anything I did that was creditable merely caused my parents to feel their loss more keenly. So I grew up with little confidence in myself."

2. Nikola enjoyed the activity of swimming from a young age and eventually became a certified lifeguard. But as a youth, he once swam too close to a dam in his local village, got pulled underneath a stone ledge, and nearly drowned.

(In the given poetic mechanism, a polyphase sestet, the current, as in the illuminated present moment, traverses Dane, who is represented by c; therefore, it cannot traverse Nikola, represented by c_1, but leaves him nil until the magnetic poles switch, which will occur on the next page. At that time, c_1 will then be traversed by maximum current and c, in turn, will fall nil. N and S represent the alternating magnetic polarities, which are progressively shifted in the commutator [as revolutionized by Nikola] to help produce polyphase currents.)

Suppose I Had Witnest a Funeral ⊂ A Peculiar Affliction

—from Nikola Ṭesla to his brother, Dane—

S

c_1

Caused by what, no one can say, ghostly objects[3] have cost
you, as me, so much youth.
Mirage of what a word referred to (sometimes a mouth) would flare before our eyes. (Sometimes a marriage.)
Reels of an internal nature fused over time, for Father taught us to make real
the consciousness of another within us, pronounced the reading of minds a sacred science.
"Син," Dane, is a part you still play. Here, I pronounce you "son," not "seen."

c · c

Son at whose feet set Father's sun: not I. From your absence rose each season & comparison.
Cast me as a servant of The Word, he did—tried. (His memories of you were costly.)
Sighing, I concede science yet fails to explain how your exquisite conscience coursed through me. And I curse the silence
reality made of you, though, really,
you made every effort of my own seem—I'll say it—*frail*, for all my youth.
My rage remains for the future, so I'll rid my eyes of yesterday, your mirage.

c_1

N

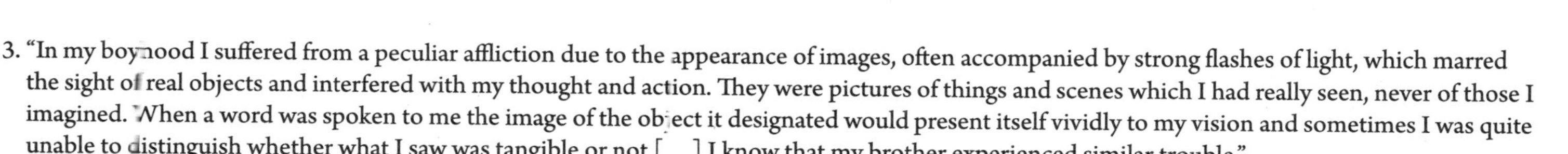

3. "In my boyhood I suffered from a peculiar affliction due to the appearance of images, often accompanied by strong flashes of light, which marred the sight of real objects and interfered with my thought and action. They were pictures of things and scenes which I had really seen, never of those I imagined. When a word was spoken to me the image of the object it designated would present itself vividly to my vision and sometimes I was quite unable to distinguish whether what I saw was tangible or not [. . .] I know that my brother experienced similar trouble."
—Nikola Tesla, *My Inventions*

Abstinence Was Not Always to Your Liking ⊂ Reading Necrologues in Vienna

—from Dane Tesla to his brother, Nikola—

N

c

Tender me a bother, but your nerve endings have tended,
since birth, to be temperamental as sin.
(Distance, brother, tempers this stance.)
Temptations dog you differently.[4] You shudder in the presence of pearls, which tamper with your sense, tempt
a door in you to slam. I see your actions performed in triplet; saw, for a time, how a gamble was all you adored.
I'll admit, Mother cast her pearls before you, knowing only guilt could cure your ill.

c_1 . c_1

Ill-suited to shooting, smoking, & making love, you seem damned to wander the city's concrete aisles,
attending time's leisure without prospect of tender or tenderness.
Adorning the future with energy intrigues you more, shutting the door
on the cinders war would turn us into. But you're not so different from me, filled with absence instead of medicines.
Attempts at indoor tempests come and go—tempers, too, though no temptresses. Your study burns, lighting the night, & sans contempt
a stanza of life rewrites itself. In your sleep you say, but only to me, "I'll be the one to annihilate distance."

c

S

4. Following are a few quotes from Niko, pulled from *My Inventions*:

"At a certain age I contracted a mania for gambling which greatly worried my parents. To sit down to a game of cards was for me the quintessence of pleasure [. .] I had a strong resolve but my philosophy was bad."

"I had a violent aversion against the earrings of women but other ornaments, as bracelets, pleased me more or less according to design. The sight of a pearl would almost give me a fit but I was fascinated with the glitter of crystals or objects with sharp edges and plane surfaces. I would not touch the hair of other people except, perhaps, at the point of a revolver. I would get a fever by looking at a peach."

"All repeated acts or operations I performed had to be divisible by three[i] and if I mist I felt impelled to do it all over again, even if it took hours."

i. When stressed, I'll repeat an action, like turning a light on and off. My "magic" number for such repetitions is four. Tesla's was three. (My parents initially planned to name me Dane; they believed I would be a boy.)

With Ease, and You Beside

There's a theory of consciousness on　　my mind & it makes me　　insecure,
states a scene within　a scene's what sets me
　　　　apart from marmosets & not　　this hard-won sinecure.

The wormwood in my ear was put there by a well-　　read poltergeist who thought
ill of the liver, grew　　livid at my writing a single-act　　play called *Venus Deferred*.

A man named Stelarc's installed a true　blue ear in his arm, & you　can listen online
to him getting held　　up at Security, a stranger's gloved finger gliding
　　　　over his glistening lobe—this　　touch, a kind of whisper.

There's a spider can run quickly as a thought, or so　　I like to think. A trap
door or a huntsman's what you'd call　　　　this arthropodal expert in allure.

Buried in axon　　　hillocks, my quantum elation takes　　　pause, prepares
to pollinate an inner space in which
　　　　neurotransmissive drift is merely a translation of *endure*.

I'm waiting to speak　　my mind, sell my quondam self
　　　　　　　　out, as if I were proof
of beauty's obscenity, as if I were　　　　　　　a Dane & knew my cure.

[To a Strange, Hollow, and Confused Noise, They Heavily Vanish]

By now, we've all heard,
		the worst is over
or like a kingdom
		yet to come, the grammar of terracide and Irish
goodbyes rinsing our tongues,
		which, if we're being honest, do not wag
with cradle songs the way they used to.
		So the infinite's a jar
emptied of anecdotes. So
		the stars are a jargon
dying of well-lit streets. I too am at a loss
		for worlds and can only let slip
I have occurred
		like a curse cured finally of itself—or
just a thought. Most places I love are
		gone, it's true,
but we can still visit them
		in a sense, in a word. This very spot once lived on
a wind-thrown stone
		that doubled as a map
of where not to go. It was emptied
		of us and therefore full
of dunes and demons,
		bogs and bleeding trees.
Did they also fail to leave
		their rapturous mark? To mask
what granules had gone missing
		from their song? I recognize

it's impossible to tell
        anything, even the hour,
in a room so "alive,"
        all reverb and verboten hope,
a billion echoes trying their best to agree
        the void adores us and that's why
it keeps on stroking our faces
        like they're lyres. Meanwhile,
the sun keeps rising
        from stage right
like an obedient paper doll; the future
        still rhymes imperfectly with horror;
and all our applause—
        like the storms we play
to put ourselves so sound to sleep—
        has finally been compressed
just into *loss*.

Geode

—for Jim Galvin

My friend brought me
one of you, said
we could crack you
open like an egg,
swaddle you in a towel
& toss you off the roof.
But then we sat turning
you over in our hands,
which you left dusty.
"Potato stone," we'd call you
if we lived across the sea,
but the sea is far
from here. We surmised
your skin is sandstone,
the breath you are
built around volcanic.
We could only guess
at what birthstone
might line you. Perhaps
peridot, green as a summer
cornfield that cuts
you if you run too swiftly
through it. Or maybe
a miniature glacier
of aquamarine stays cool
in your depths despite
our warm palms. Were we
wrong to think we'd be better

off if we were more like you—
earthlike as your name,
humble as a paperweight,
our glamor swallowed up
in our thick skin? There
are versions of you whole
people can stand
inside. A farmer
in Ohio once harvested
light from your walls,
the kind we launch
into certain nights
to say "this is new"
or to rally old feelings
of freedom, you might say.
But that farmer is long
buried & his hollowed
bit of glittering
earth is a roadside attraction
few know to adore. You
say so little, making us
ashamed of all the noise
we bathe you in. We knock at you
as if you were
a door behind which hides
the shape of some god's
sigh. We know fancy folks
who'd pay to hold
your contents to their temples
or their lips, thinking you full
of powers said
to heal, make strong
or wise or fertile. We resist

the temptation to form
a nest of straw
around you, find a hen
to heat you into opening. Instead,
we hold you to our ears,
as if we could hear
a millennium breaking
into song or years.

My Invention

There in the feral neon of night,
I carried my tune like a torch

Invention itself had finally eclipsed.
Still, I carried it, even after all the moths

Lost interest and moved on
To more convincing decoy moons:

See them hover martial in their lines—
Street lamps, porch lamps, the concrete plains

Of parking lots made consecrate with snow,
Stained orange in their towering

Low-watt glares. The tune

∴

I've lost it now, carried

                    Away as I am
By the Earth's emulation

Of lunar desolations spied by spacecraft—
Deep craters you want to crawl into

For the taste of hope. Two turns
Of the century ago, hope was just a lamp

Filled with oil, drawn from a whale
Few people knew how to draw

With any accuracy. Back then, reading lines
Late into the industrial

Night made you a lucubrator, soul
Dependent on the leviathan's

Bulbed head, your gold light lifted
From a still-warm sac

He used to hear his compatriots' songs.

∴

Such music, it turned out,
Was extinguishable: Harpoons

Grew rusty in their corners. Illumination
Now caught

By riskier means.
Dynamos. Wires. Filaments

Afloat in blown glass orbs.
Chairs that could light

Your whole mind on fire. In 1847,
A stagehand takes a single

Lamentable step into the new
Current—and falls

Insensate upon contact with such power,
His singed ghost given up

Within the hour. Little question as to whether

∴

The show has gone on. Even now,
I swivel in my chair under a bulb

It burns my eyes to look at—so I don't.
So I drag my cursor's blinking "I"

Over a lesser light, a window-
Sized expanse so blue

You'd think it was mimicking
The sea. In 1956, Mao Zedong

Pens a poem called "Swimming,"
Detailing his wettest dream to dam

The Yangtze, redirect its ancient, civilization-
Causing course. (See the engineers,

Less critical of the poem
Than its subject, subject

To imprisonment for their tastes.) But light
And its shifty mechanisms—aren't they also

Oddly lovely? Li Bai wandering alone
along a river, drunk on wine and the distant

Dynasty of moonlight in his hands. A dying chameleon
Clutching a twig on the jungle floor, also alone,

Adrift in the centuries, prismatic flesh in full finale . . . Teals
Flashing, throbbing pointillism of fuchsias and greens

Vanishing in a majesty
Outside of history. Or Loïe

Fuller twirling in her skirts,
Her proto-cinematic silks lit from beneath—

∴

And changing

Color as she turns, radiantly
Turns, relentless

As a Tesla dynamo, arms beating
Up and down, the theater its own magnetic field of

Vision. Of course, Tesla nearly died
Swimming as a boy

In Smiljan, where his brilliant
Mother recited Serbian epic

Poetry to him, even as he stroked
The local cats, coaxing electricity

From their dark fur. The town's river
One day overwhelms him, is what I am

Trying to say, conveys him
Toward a would-be-fatal

Fall: Only by clawing
His way along the grim corroded lip

Of an old dam, angling his body
Bladelike against the current, is he able

To save himself—and his future
"All-seeing eye." (Picture its laser gaze

Scanning the Earth, first poem it will commit
To memory, until

All opacities yield to optics, and even our most
Buried flames fail to stay secret.)

∴

On my screen, I see you
Now can buy a mask that gorges

Your pores on therapeutic light, deletes
Each telling line before

It turns your face
Into a poem. The dream

Of deterring
Time is not so current, I think. In 1917,

In New Jersey, young women start to draw
Radium-dusted brushes betwixt

Their lips, making fine the points
Of their instruments, which they cant

Like fragile gnomons in their hands,
Dabbing green illumination on

Watch faces, also control
Panels of aircraft. (See them gleam

In the war-torn night, brushstrokes of flame
Unnaming the sky.) Maybe

The women see their workplace as a spa,
Since people pay

Dearly in such decades just to bathe
In radium, therapy only

The wealthy can enjoy, their skeletons
Not yet aware

Of death's cruel imprecision,
How bones can live and turn to dust

At the same time, a tooth put off light
Even after buried

In the earth. In 2009, the Earth
Slows very slightly—so slightly

Even a worm cannot feel it,
Our sphere's

Song shifting infinitesimally
Toward largo. (In *Inferno*,

Dante calls hell's light
Infected.) And the poles

Contract, our diurnal
Turn grows slightly more

Labored, hesitant in the name
Of a growing need

For efficient, modern, power-
Generating dams, like the epic Three

Gorges Dam—or the muse
Of "Swimming."

∴

("My head is swimming," is a thing
We sometimes say when overwhelmed,

To indicate language is a liquid
That might drown you,

If you let it, out for all of time.)

∴

Sometimes a certain
Slant of light takes

Over, and one is thrown
Into a scene pre-

Historic in nature, in which a man,
Donning clothes made of the same

Hide as his frail walls, observes dawn
Both as malignancy and magic, streaming

In as it is through a fatal wound
That once transformed a land

Mammal into shelter, clothing, food,
And weaponry. Light veritably floods

Through this flesh's
Aperture, ushering

The wilderness
Inside, plashing it perfectly

Upside down on the oppo-
Site wall, while our first

Photographer overflows
With distress and wonder,

Pressing two fingers to the tear,
As if to staunch this flow

Of what is, and is not, there.

∴

I forget the year
In which I play a shade in the ballet

La Bayadere, my arabesque a fragile link
In the wan chain descending

The stage, raked and reifying
An invented man's ethereal

Invention. (That I am
Identically postured as the girl

Both preceding and following me
Might be a form of pleasure

For a person I'll never meet—
Spectacles glinting in the dark

Auditorium we call "the house.")
There is a shade in my house

Which lowers at the command
Direct sunlight is programmed to be. The idea

Being the shade will guard our art
And furnishings (also a red-hued floor

Whose source once breathed and bent,
Phototropic, in tropical winds before sustaining

Incisions in the name
Of animé—sap that soothes

The lung, perfumes the wrist, and finishes
So many surfaces) from ultra-

Violent rays. Also activated,
This shade, by your voice.

∴

(In Rome, under the reign
Of Augustus, Virgil writes

"Robbed of light" to express
What happens to a body when it's executed.)

∴

What if we were marine

Creatures that could mate just by lingering
In the same thin element, however

Briefly, never actually
Touching, like the nerve

Endings in our cortices, enticed
To spark—

See *filament* give way
To *lament*—a thought,

And coming so close . . .
Eerie eros in a pinch of space. Picture

Our shared ceiling of water
Netted with light, our voices

Rising between our faces, tiny beads
Glinting with emptiness.

∴

In the year of the plague,
My husband markets light. Dimmer

Switches, more exactly. Also, shades.
He's very good at it.

You should hear his pitch.
He'll tell you light is the protagonist

Of every story, even your own.
This arc of light calls to mind

A certain type of soil-
Loving nematode, of which the males

Glow blue while their bodies
Unlearn this life, a phenomenon

Known as "death
Fluorescence." May I be nothing

But a pinch of blue light
When this poem reaches you

To tell you there were still stories
In its unrelenting day,

Of a waterfall salmon once climbed:
Before their greatest river

Was revised, they were thought of
As people, and you could walk

Right over the raging
Current on their flashing backs.

The touch of your soles could not even
Demean them. In a picture I have pinned

Above my desk, a man
Stands grayly over this very fall,

A hoop of net extended into space, his huge catch
All but catching itself

In the mist and the light
And the net. Meanwhile, Mao dreams on . . .

Perfecting his back stroke, singing
To a mountain goddess, *if she is still there to hear,*

Of the great plans afoot: chasms turned
To thoroughfares, whole weather systems

Tamed between two walls,
And night detained, so it might learn

How long the day might finally grow.

Cell + Thief

I.

I have held hell up
to the light, had my Hadean
globe filled with glitter-water,
blissless & bitter virago
called I. All blood ballad
when I wind it up, let it play—
lyricless—back to me, a verse
that sheds itself like yesterday's derma
on the sheets. I'm not averse to being
reborn an imago
limited to holding an edible blade,
unable to plea innocent,
indelible. I've never been
well nor versed
in wealth, only in the feeling
I'm fleeing called *less,* called
listless. Yes, I'm a go, I'm down
to accompany you into this earth
that doesn't ask to be
remembered or reversed. Together
we'll dismantle every devil
that's ever lived
inside a skull, require this dream
to last like the memory of learning
the planets were once a choir.

II.

I can't place
your voice, so I replace my own. I
keep it penned
with the Gadarenes
in the backyard. They're always hungry & full
of ire. The emperor wants to fire the planet. The tea
is cold. Everyone is spent,
unable to save
anything but *up*, which is where we've sent
the children, the squires,
& the insane—because the future is worth
it & Mars has come a long way, hell-
bent as it is on being acquired. According
to Yeats, time moves in
the double image of a gyre,
spiraling through limit to arrive
at limit deferred. Let's take the day
off, our slips too. Let's blend
ourselves a Lethean tonic. I'll propose
& you'll say, *Yes, you are the mean and I
the end.*

III.

We descend by twos into the chthonic promised
land, where oxygen quits
us, our ilk
finally the chronic *all* that's lived
without—pallid, blind beneath
our feet, unable to fend
off the earthquake of a single step.
Water drips like milk
from the ceiling until it becomes
a straw, a dagger, an agatoid curtain. I've sinned
every second
of your life, but like the caterpillar fallen
into Xi Ling-shi's tea to birth silk,
I don't witness
the necessity of my own invention, filamentous
end. I wasn't born to
mind, be resigned
as the birth certificate of a stiff or the blood-
blank portrait I draw
daily in the name of inducing
unlabored breath & awe.

IV.

It's raw, this knee too used
to kneeling, this throat too used to urging
God toward bellicose
ends. Let's be friends—because I can't
treat my enemy as anything
but me. I fasten my bra,
hook hooks into eyes
meant for a narrower cage. One lives
by these minor afflictions, their otiose
inflections, the immaculate patterning of
flaw. Every time I break
out my awl,
it's to pierce these loose boots
so their tongues don't flap like failure's flag.
A daughter owes
her mother something, so I don't go out in public
looking like hell. Cell + thief =
self, I say, my maw
glistening & agape, no law to its name, no
latticework of ancestry to climb. Just a lonely
fable, passed down from God-Knows-Whom,
about a womb that wandered
until able—

Paradise Lust

Myth informs me you have need   of neither foot nor wing, bird-of-paradise.
Yet you remain aloft, & when you land, you're pure   lustrum, cured of paradise.

Soon I'll glimpse the constellated   you, your body a bending
                    arrow in austral skies;
but for now, I'll keep confiding   in the night: I need a word with paradise.

It's 1910. Milliners immortalize your plumes, turn your tussocked tail to frill,
your evolution to adornment. What spills   from ribboned brims: denatured   paradise.

I watch you bloom—xanthous, aliform, inviting. Though your pollinator's feet were
pared away, my fingers find your spathe, spread   what is no longer
                                        measured by paradise.

Passeriforme, formal—you dance the way others breathe. Thought to breed in mid-
air, to pass at the earth's touch, your love is a thing lured   by paradise.

It's 2033 & you're growing   on my mother's southern grave, under the name
Strelitzia. I planted you believing your pulchritude   perennial, inured to paradise.

Your name is rootbound with royal,   form & enclosure. I slip off my
shoes, take a walk through polyandriums nightly   marred by paradise.

This game of lost & found is leaving me   troubled & teased. Walker, your feet are
bare & your hands hold nothing but mire. Your mind   is going absurd with paradise.

Notes

A number of the poems in this collection were originally drafted in ottava rima, sestina, and other classical forms that, in the drafting process, became—through relineation, repatterning, deletions and substitutions, rearrangements of rhymes, etc.—eroded beyond immediate recognition.

Morsels from the notebook in which "The Perch" was first drafted:

> *By what purge?*
> *What is the tenor of your tragedy*
> —OEDIPUS, Sophocles's *Oedipus Rex* (translated by Sir George Young)
>
> *Every fish is from a form*
> *of underworld.*
> —a line from an early draft of "The Perch"
>
> *Tears in the eyes of a fish*
> —MATSUO BASHŌ (translated by Robert Hass)

The epigraphs from "Glossolaliac" are taken from Roland Barthes's *The Pleasure of the Text* and 1 Corinthians 14:2, respectively. The poem is addressed to a version of the ancient Sumerian god, Enlil, for whose name "Lord Storm" serves as a translation.

"Australopitheca & Starman" is a modern translation of, and reply to, Sir Philip Sidney's famous Petrarchan sonnet series, "Astrophil and Stella," whose speaker is "Astrophil" ("Star Lover") and whose object of obsession is "Stella" ("star"), a personification-in-female-form of the heavens themselves—with all their intoxicating implications of immortality and fate. But what if Stella spoke back—and at length? And what if rather than being heavenly, she were earthly, the most earthly of humans you might imagine? An actual fossil buried in the earth? And what if Astrophil were not merely a *lover* of stars but their eternal companion, a fellow prisoner of distance?

From these questions sprang into being this countdown-of-a-crown of sonnets. The spellings of words are somewhat nonstandard, combining Sidney's own original spellings with those presently used in modern SMS language or "text speak."

The translation of Dante in the epigraph for "Crown Shyness" is my own, since I didn't find an existing English translation that attended to Dante's Latin scholarship—aka his presumable knowledge that the verb *scerpere* (*scerpare* in modern Italian), "to rend or tear off," derives from the Latin, *excerpere,* "to choose."

"Crown Shyness" was originally drafted in 2020 (in Brooklyn) as a crown of sonnets; subsequently, though, I pruned it.

"[Horns Within]" takes its title from a stage direction in William Shakespeare's *The Tragedie of King Lear,* a direction that puns off of an insult The Fool directs at Lear, casting the king as a snail (a symbol of cuckoldry and devilishness, among other things).

"Ode to Your Majesty" draws its epigraph from "Poema XIII" of Pablo Neruda's *Veinte poemas de amor y una canción desesperada.*

"As a Prisoner for the Lord, Then, I Urge You to Live" takes its title from Ephesians 4:1.

"Paris Green" is in the voice of Mary Ann Cotton, Britain's first convicted female serial killer. She was executed by hanging. The title is derived from Cotton's attorney's defensive claim that she did not poison her children and husbands with arsenic, but rather that the arsenic-based colorant in a popular "Paris green" wallpaper at the time was responsible for their violent and untimely deaths. She is thought to have poisoned and killed between thirteen and twenty-one people.

"The New Pastoralism" is a villanelle that takes cues from a series of models and essays, originally published in *Architectural Digest* 223, that sought to mend the gap between the pastoral and the futuristic, the green and the biomimetic, the nostalgic and the cybernetic. "Green" was meaningfully conflated with Romanticism within the context of the digest's folio.

The epigraph opening section II uses Edward Snow's translation of Rainer Maria Rilke's *Duino Elegies.*

"[Enter Hero]" takes its title from a stage direction in Shakespeare's *Much Ado About Nothing.*

"Optimal Stopping" refers to a type of math problem, two famous examples of which are the "secretary problem" and the "sultan problem."

"The Euthanasia Coaster" was inspired by Lithuanian artist Julijonas Urbonas's PhD thesis (for the Royal College of Art in London), which consists of a roller coaster design that, if reified, would supply passengers with a euphoric exodus from this life, the ride's extreme and sustained centrifugal force and velocity inducing fatal hypoxia. The poem is a modified (uncurled) sestina or "septima," since it has seven- instead of six-lined stanzas.

"Voice Over" plays with the origin of voice-over as a technological response to oceangoing vessels' need for wireless communication. Later, of course, it was adapted to artistic use in radio and film, a famous early example being Walt Disney's *Steamboat Willie.*

The two photographs of Thomas Edward Lawrence included in "Citadel" are in the public domain. The first photo is sourced from Nasjonalbiblioteket via picryl.com, the second from Lowell Thomas's *With Lawrence in Arabia* (Hutchinson & Co., London, 1924).

"With Ease, and You Beside" was written with Emily Dickinson and Gerald Edelman, author of neuronal group selection theory, in mind.

"[To a Strange, Hollow, and Confused Noise, They Heavily Vanish]" is a stage direction in Shakespeare's *The Tempest.*

The tree referenced in "My Invention" is *Hymenaea courbaril,* also known as Brazilian copal.

Acknowledgments

Grateful acknowledgment is made to Milkweed Editions and to the editors of the following publications: Your faith is a fuel to contemporary writers and readers alike. Many thanks, as well, to the ghosts of Amy Lowell and Carolyn Moore, whose shared love of poetry continues to redefine the possible.

This book is in loving memory of Michael Claude Koch (1947–2022), whose mentorship was nothing short of life-saving. A world without him is a world deprived.

American Poetry Review: "Cell + Thief," "As a Prisoner for the Lord, Then, I Urge You to Live," "Australopitheca & Starman," "Crown Shyness," "Desert Theater," "My Invention," "The Perch"

Bennington Review: "Ode to 'Your Majesty'"

Blackbird: "Paradise Lust"

Conduit: "[Enter Hero]," "Lazarus Species," "Voice Over"

DIAGRAM: "The New Pastoralism"

Iowa Review: "The Euthanasia Coaster"

Lana Turner: "Glossolaliac," "With Ease, and You Beside"

Los Angeles Review of Books: "C. Elegans," "[Horns Within]"

The Nation: "Formalwear," "Optimal Stopping"

The New York Review of Books: "[To a Strange, Hollow, and Confused Noise, They Heavily Vanish]"

Ninth Letter: "Scrap"

Southampton Review: "Geode"

Poet Lore: "Paris Green"

Poet's Country: "Abacus & Doubt"

Poetry Society of America: "Noise Cancelling" (recipient of the 2021 Lucille Medwick Memorial Prize)

The Rumpus: "Ameliorates"

West Branch Wired: "Vacancy"

Zyzzyva: "My Madness Is My Love Toward Mankind"

DEVON WALKER-FIGUEROA is the author of *Philomath*, which won the National Poetry Series and the Levis Reading Prize, and was a finalist for the National Book Critics Circle's John Leonard Prize. A former Amy Lowell Traveling Scholar, Walker-Figueroa is an assistant professor of English at Virginia Commonwealth University.

milkweed
EDITIONS

Founded as a nonprofit organization in 1980, Milkweed Editions is an independent publisher. Our mission is to identify, nurture, and publish transformative literature, and build an engaged community around it.

We are based in Bde Óta Othúŋwe (Minneapolis) in Mní Sota Makhóčhe (Minnesota), the traditional homeland of the Dakhóta and Anishinaabe (Ojibwe) people and current home to many thousands of Dakhóta, Ojibwe, and other Indigenous people, including four federally recognized Dakhóta nations and seven federally recognized Ojibwe nations.

We believe all flourishing is mutual, and we envision a future in which all can thrive. Realizing such a vision requires reflection on historical legacies and engagement with current realities. We humbly encourage readers to do the same.

milkweed.org

Milkweed Editions, an independent nonprofit literary publisher, gratefully acknowledges sustaining support from our board of directors, the McKnight Foundation, the National Endowment for the Arts, and many generous contributions from foundations, corporations, and thousands of individuals—our readers. This activity is made possible by the voters of Minnesota through a Minnesota State Arts Board Operating Support grant, thanks to a legislative appropriation from the Arts and Cultural Heritage Fund.

Interior design by Alex Guerra
Typeset in Arno

Arno was designed by Robert Slimbach. Slimbach named this typeface after the river that runs through Florence, Italy. Arno draws inspiration from a variety of typefaces created during the Italian Renaissance; its italics were inspired by the calligraphy and printing of Ludovico degli Arrighi.